Lock+Load

WEAPONS OF THE US MILITARY

Lock+Load

WEAPONS OF THE US MILITARY

Angus Konstam • Jerry Scutts • Hans Halberstadt • Simon Forty
• Leo Marriott

PRC

Produced in 2002 by
PRC Publishing Ltd,
64 Brewery Road, London N7 9NT

A member of Chrysalis Books plc

Published in the U.S. and Canada by:
Sterling Publishing Co., Inc.
387 Park Avenue South
New York, NY 10016

ISBN 1 85648 634 6

Printed and bound in China

Acknowledgments by Simon Forty

The US Army and Center of Military History web sites provide an excellent overview of the history and current readiness of the US Army. The army section of Lock and Load is based primarily on the information provided on these websites, in such material as the pamphlet *225 Years of Service* by Brigadier General John S. Brown, Chief of Military History at the US Army's Center of Military History and by material supplied by Hans Halberstadt who is individually credited for his photographs.

Getting photographs in the field is always a team effort, with the photographer simply the front end of a bunch of helpful people who helped him get in a position to point his lens at the right places. Among the many who helped me I'd like to single out LTC Ricardo Riera, CPT Pete Fedak, CPT Charles Greene, CPT Reggie Salazar, SSG Lerolland, SFC Tony Bowen, PV2 Lawren Slockish, PFC William Oliver, SGT Israel Matez, SSG Christopher Dumont, SGT Robert Birchenough, PFC Martens, PFC Garza, SPC Merrill, SPC Adam, PFC Cira, SPC Richter, SPC Horton.

CONTENTS

ABBREVIATIONS

A

AAA Anti-aircraft Artillery
AC Active Component
ACC Air Combat Command
ADCAP Advanced Capability
AIC Action Information Center
ALCM Air Launched Cruise Missile
ALWT Advanced Lightweight Torpedo
APC Armored Personnel Carrier
ARNG Army Reserve National Guard
ASM Air-to-surface Missile
ASV Armored Security Vehicle
ASW Antisubmarine Warfare
ATACMS Army Tactical Missile System
AVLB Armored Vehicle Launched Bridge

B

BFIST Bradley Fire Support Vehicle
BPDMS Basic Point Defense Missile System

C

CAP Combat Air Patrol
CBIRF Chemical Biological Incident Response Force
CCIP Common Configuration Implementation Program
CIC Combat Information Center
CIWS Close In Weapon System
CMM Conventional Munitions Module0
CRT Cathode Ray Tube

D

DPICM Dual-purpose Improved Conventional Munition
DSMAC Digital Scene-matching Area Correlator

E

ECM Electronic Counter Measures
ER Extended Range
ERGM Extended Range Guided Munition

F

F&F Fire and forget
FAST Fleet Anti-terrorism Security Teams
FCS Fire Control System
FCS Fire Control System
FLIR Forward Looking Infrared
FMTV Family of Medium Tactical Vehicles

ABBREVIATIONS

G

GPS Global Positioning System

GWMS Guided Missile Weapons System

H

HEDP High Explosive Dual Purpose

HMMWV High Mobility Multipurpose Wheeled Vehicle

HQDA Headquarters, Department of the Army

I

IFV/CFV Infantry/Cavalry fighting vehicles

INS Inertial Navigation System

IR/UV infrared/ultraviolet

J

JDAM Joint Direct Attack Munitions

JSF Joint Strike Fighter

JVC Jet Vane Control

L

LBE Load Bearing Equipment

LO Low-observable

LOSAT Line-of-sight Anti-tank

M

MAGTF Marine Air-Ground Task Forces

MLRS Multi-launch Rocket System

MMS Mast-mounted Sight

MOS Military Occupation Speciality

MPRS Multipoint Refueling System

MR Medium Range

MRE Meal, Ready to Eat

N

NSFS Naval Surface Fire Support

NSSMS NATO Sea Sparrow Missile System

NTC National Training Center

O

OICW Objective Individual Combat Weapon

OPEVAL Operational Evaluations

OTH-T Over-the-horizon-targeting

P

PGM Precision Guided Munition

R

RAM Radar Absorbent Material or Rolling Airframe Missile

RC Reserve Component

RPG Rocket-propelled Grenade

RPV Remotely Piloted Vehicle

RSTA Reconnaissance, Surveillance, and Target Acquisition

S

SAM Surface-to-air Missile

SAR Search and Rescue

SAW Squad Automatic Weapon

SDD System Development and Demonstration

SLAM Stand-off Land Attack Missile

STOVL Short Take-off Vertical Landing

T

TAC Tactical Air Command

TAINS TERCOM Assisted Inertial Navigation System

TBMD Theatre Ballistic Missile Defense

TDD Target Detection Device

TOW Tube-launched, Optically-tracked, Wire-guided Missile

TSAAM Tri-Service Stand Off Attack Missile

TUAV Tactical Unmanned Aerial Vehicle

U

UBFCS Underwater Battery Fire Control System

UCAV Unmanned Combat Air Vehicle

USAR(C) US Army Reserve (Command)

V

VTO Vertical Take-off

INTRODUCTION

The production of military weaponry is a necessity in a hostile world. Events such as the attacks of September 11, 2001 on New York and Washington DC, and the recent conflicts in Afghanistan, Iraq, the Balkans, and the Middle East underline the necessity that the United States of America's armed forces stand in readiness for any future conflict, anywhere in the world. At the height of the Cold War, the United State's military was equipped and trained to fight the Warsaw Pact, particularly the armed forces of the Soviet Union. This meant countering the large Soviet nuclear submarine fleet with an antisubmarine capability, spearheaded by the US Navy's nuclear attack submarines. The almost overwhelming numbers of Soviet tanks on the East German border where matched with fewer but better tanks, and with mechanized infantry with a powerful antitank capability. Air-supremacy fighters were developed that were designed to stop the massed ranks of Soviet strike aircraft from reaching their NATO targets. Above all there was a massive commitment to military spending, weapons development and procurement, and in the development of military technology.

All this changed with the end of the Cold War. For the last decade, the United States has been trying to redefine the role of its armed forces, and attempting to decide just what level of military spending is appropriate in an age where the United States of America is the world's only superpower. The change in role from Cold War protagonist to post-Cold War "world policeman" (if indeed that is an appropriate new role) was not an easy process, and indeed, was not the result of a planned strategy. Increasing involvement in peacekeeping forays into the Third World and in former Yugoslavia mandated this new responsibility. Before, America's involvement in Third World affairs had been colored by its role as a Cold War superpower. In the last decade, this changed to one where its armed forces sought to ensure stability, order, and democratic rule if called upon to do so. This meant a change in the way troops, aircraft, ships, and weapons systems were employed, and it also led to a significant change in

RIGHT: A Marine assault amphibious vehicle comes ashore at Port Ploce in Croatia.

SFOR
SFOR

old methods of weapons demand and procurement. Put simply, the American military needed to reequip itself and retrain its forces in order to carry out its new role. The commencement of the "War on Terrorism" found the American military largely unprepared for the scale of commitment it was required to undertake. Its fleet had gone through a relatively simple conversion process, with an increasing emphasis on naval airpower and amphibious capabilities rather than attack submarines or antiship capabilities. For the US Air Force, the new demands placed a great strain on a service that was used to operating in certain theaters, and from well-established bases. It now had to devise ways in which its aircraft could operate in new far-flung theaters of war such as Afghanistan, and where its opponent lacked the relatively sophisticated antiaircraft capability of the former Soviet Union. As for the US Army, it was still locked into its commitment to maintain powerful mechanized and armored formations, while its new role demanded the deployment of rapid reaction forces of lightly equipped infantry.

The aim of this book is to outline the arsenal available to the American military in this crucial period in its development, and to explain how effective it is in any current or future conflict. To begin, we must assess the effectiveness of the arms of the American military machine, and examine how its changing role affects its choice and employment of weaponry.

The Changing Role of the Post-Cold War American Military Machine

If an American general was asked what the future held for the US military in 1985, he would be sure of his role, and that of the men who served him. He would know the effectiveness of the weapons at his disposal, and of the way they would be used in combat if the need arose. His enemy was the Warsaw Pact, principally the Soviet Union. Although he might cast condescending remarks at the lower level of technology enjoyed by his Soviet foes, he would retain a certain unease at the numbers of troops, tanks, and aircraft which could be arrayed against his own forces. At the time, the United States was supposed to enjoy a technological advantage in military terms over the Soviet Union. American submarines were quieter and more deadly, its tanks more powerful, and its fighter aircraft more advanced. Then, a new generation of Soviet weapons systems emerged, such as the MiG-29 fighter-bomber, or the Typhoon Class nuclear ballistic-missile submarine (SSBN). There is a certain truth in the old adage that quality is better than quantity. The Soviets had also proven in the closing days of World War II that quantity has a quality all of its own. These next-generation weapons systems threatened to close the technological gap, while the quantity difference was maintained. This alarming situation continued for another couple of years, until events, which the American military might have thought unthinkable, actually happened. The Cold War ended. Virtually overnight the military stand-off which had existed for four decades was ended, to be replaced by uncertainty, both in terms of world stability and in the future role of the US military.

While the Pentagon was still coming to terms with these dramatic changes, and was facing the prospect of a spectacularly curtailed defense budget, the United States became embroiled in the first conflict fought (in the words of President Bush Sr) on behalf of "the New World Order." The invasion of Kuwait by the forces of President Saddam Hussein of Iraq was seen as an unacceptable act of aggression, and invited the condemnation of the United Nations, followed by a military response. In the Gulf War which followed, American armored divisions, mechanized groups, airborne forces, and Marines fought a conventional war, albeit one preceded by a hitherto unimaginable demonstration of firepower. In a matter of days, the air forces of the United States and its UN allies broke the will of the Iraqi army to fight, decimated its air force and launched strikes against Iraq's command, supply, and transport networks. Warships of the US Navy pounded Iraqi positions using gunfire, and battleships reequipped with cruise

ABOVE, RIGHT: A line of M60A1 tanks and support vehicles at a staging area North of Karlsruhe, Germany.

RIGHT: M60A1 tanks on the inspection line at Rhine Ordnance near Kaiserslautern, Germany. The M60 MBT was the mainstay of US Army armored units for most of the 1970s and 1980s before it was replaced by the M1 Abrams.

missiles launched attacks as far away as Baghdad; a remorseless pounding that demonstrated the firepower available to the US military, and its ability to strike virtually at will wherever it chooses. The ground war which followed was something of an anticlimax, as despite some pockets of heavy resistance, the Iraqi army melted in the face of the allied offensive against it. The war was a clear demonstration that the "New World Order" had teeth, but it also showed that conventional doctrines and political constraints shackled it. President Bush was criticized for not continuing the war, and "finishing off Saddam," but he had no other option, given the political constraints of the UN resolution which had permitted him to assemble his coalition of forces in the first place.

In the ten years following the Gulf War, the US military and successive American governments tried to come to terms with the realities of the post-Cold War world. With no real need to maintain a massive military presence in Europe and in the North Atlantic, the services underwent a process known as "downsizing;" bases were closed, servicemen retired, budgets cut, and new projects shelved. Faced with an incredible uncertainty as to the future role of America's armed forces, strategists in the Pentagon were hard-pressed to decide what shape the future American war machine would take. Even though decisions about the future of research projects, weapons units, and manpower levels were hard to take, given the lack of hard information available as to the future facing America's fighting men and women, the government and the Pentagon had even tougher decisions to make.

At the height of the Cold War, the United States and the Soviet Union both maintained a nuclear arsenal that was capable of destroying all life on Earth several times over. Given that the Cold War was over, and the threat of nuclear war had receded, what was to happen to the nuclear arsenal; the

BELOW: Corporal Carlos Rivera uses a satellite phone to establish communications from the field in the village of Skugrici, Bosnia and Herzegovina, in 1999.

LEFT: A US army M-113 APC prepares to pull an armored Humvee out of the mud in Bosnia and Herzegovina, in 1996, during Operation Joint Endeavor. The spring-time mud presented a challenge to the soldiers and their equipment..

"Weapons of Mass Destruction" (WMD)? Despite wide support for non-proliferation efforts and the gradual dismantling of many Soviet missile silos, the world was not a safer place, and had not escaped the threat of a "nuclear winter." Although states such as the United Kingdom, France, and even China could be expected to abide by existing agreements, the new nuclear nations of India, Pakistan, and to a lesser extent Israel, were more of a problem as all three countries exist in near-continual state of military tension. Other countries such as Iraq or North Korea were also actively trying to gain access to nuclear weapons. The collapse of the Soviet Union also raised the specter that terrorist organizations might be able to gain access to nuclear weapons. Biological weapons were even more prevalent in the Third World, and current diplomatic initiatives had failed to enforce non-proliferation bans. Analysts were even unable to agree under what conditions the United States might use its nuclear or biological weapons in the future. One solution actively sought by successive administrations was some form of protection against rogue nuclear attacks. The "star wars" Strategic Defense Initiative (SDI) has now emerged as a potentially feasible yet extremely expensive option for the US government. The current American administration has forged ahead with the development of the SDI—despite protests from America's allies, other nuclear powers, and even its own advisors. It is also unable to protect against nuclear weapons triggered from inside US territory by terrorist groups, and is equally unable to prevent a conventional terrorist attack, such as that of September 11, 2001. Today, the recent "anthrax" scare and biological threats have made the specter of these forms of "catastrophic terrorism" more tangible than some vague missile attack from a future nuclear-armed enemy. The fate of America's nuclear arsenal is still in question, but the role of the rest of its military personnel is becoming clearer.

In the decade following the end of the Cold War, war or the threat of conflict is still commonplace around the world. Civil wars, anarchy, and insurrection are still commonplace in Africa, while drug cartels in Venezuela, rebellion in Sri Lanka, and ethnic tension in the Balkans all threaten world stability. Since the Gulf War, America has adopted the role of "world policeman" ceded by Britain in 1945. American troops have been involved in conflicts in Somalia, the Caribbean, Bosnia, Kosovo, and in the

ABOVE: A Hawk surface-to-air missile is launched during the first ever live firing using targeting data supplied by air defense radar at McGregor Range near Fort Bliss, Texas, in 1987.

RIGHT: US Marine Corps Captain Rick Uribe pulls in his parachute at the drop zone in Kuwait.

RIGHT and BELOW: US Army troops have been involved in many of the world's hot spots since the end of World War II. Today technological superiority and skills honed by realistic training – allied to excellent motivation and ésprit de corps – have produced a balanced force that can perform equally effectively in large set-piece operations and smaller mobile engagements. The most important part of this is the quality of the fighting men at the army's disposal.

Middle East. The failure of America's efforts to bring about stability in Somalia in 1993 led to a temporary end to America's involvement in its new role, but the crisis in Bosnia then Kosovo prompted a return to the head of the "New World Order." Supported by Britain and to a lesser extent other European powers, the US fought and won a war in Kosovo using the threat of ground intervention and a well-managed air campaign. This victory was inexpensive in terms of American lives, but it led to a false expectation. After Vietnam, the American public were reluctant to commit American troops to overseas theaters, and were loath to see Americans killed in actions fought far from home. This public posture had to be balanced with the strategic superiority enjoyed by the United States after the collapse of the Soviet Union. There was also its new-found position as the leader of the "New World Order" to consider; this club had also started to encompass the Russian Federation and other former enemies in a supporting role. As the self-styled "leader of the free world," the United States was unable to return to the era of isolationism

ABOVE: A jumpmaster gives a two minute warning to paratroopers as they near the drop zone.

LEFT: A soldier from the 82nd Airborne Division exits out of an Air Force C-141B Starlifter.

ABOVE, RIGHT: M1A1 Abrams main battle tanks from the US Army 1st Armored Division coordinate their fire along with two AH-64A Apache helicopters.

RIGHT: A US Marine Corps M1A1 main battle tank churns the sand as it heads up the beach after off-loading from a US Navy Landing Craft Air Cushion during amphibious training.

during the early 20th century. Like it or not, the United States was a superpower, and had to act the part. For the strategists in the Pentagon, this meant defining a role for the military in the 21st century, and determining how, where, and why troops, weapons, and resources would be deployed. This new role was just emerging when Islamic fundamentalist terrorists struck New York and Washington DC in September 2001. Overnight, the role of the American military machine had changed.

The weaponry described in this book is no longer that of a Cold War protagonist, or the tools of a "world policeman." They represent the arsenal of a nation at war with terrorism, a state locked in a struggle with a largely unseen enemy intent on its destruction.

BELOW: The AIM-9 Sidewinder infrared heat-seeking air-to-air missile is still the most important dogfighting missile available. It has proved its worth in many engagements, including the Falklands War when RAF and RN Harriers cleared the skies of Argentine aircraft.

Weapons Procurement and the American Defense Industry

For nearly 50 years since the end of World War II, the American defense industry was guaranteed orders for new weapons, funding for research, and secure jobs for its workers. The Cold War was good for the sector, and through developing links between the US military, the government, and the leading defense contractors, a continual series of new and ever-more expensive projects ensured that the United States of America maintained its technological edge over its Soviet opponents. Following the end of the Cold War and the collapse of the Soviet Union, this all changed. What followed would be a decade of uncertainty, "downsizing," and job losses as the US military cut back its commitment to military spending, and the size of its armed forces.

Even before the end of the Cold War in 1990, the weapons procurement budget of the United States military was under pressure. In real terms, US

ABOVE: The AIM-7 Sparrow is an excellent standoff weapon but has proved less effective than the Sidewinder in air combat.

RIGHT: The catapult officer gives the final okay signal to the pilot of this EA-6B Prowler to launch from the flight deck of USS *Saratoga* CV-60.

military expenditure on weaponry reached its peak in 1985. After 1990, there was a massive reduction in military effort, which in turn led to a reduction in demand for military equipment. While there is no easy yardstick against which to measure the scale of this reduction in procurement, the employment and sales figures of America's leading warship, plane, and weapon manufacturers help to identify the size of the change. Arms sales and employment levels in the largest arms producing companies fell by an average of 15 percent between 1991 and 1994, and by a further 10 percent in the following six years (1995–2000). At the start of the 21st century, there was a nationwide (if not global) uncertainty as to the nature of the future demand for military hardware. It was an industry without a goal, serving a military without direction. There are certain immovable factors, such as the need of the military to deter any

attack on the national borders and on American interests overseas, and if that fails, to defeat any aggressor. Until September 11, 2001, any further levels of commitment were subject to the vagaries of politicians and their varying levels of commitment to overseas adventures. Even after extensive American military involvement in the global war against terrorism, the requirement for military hardware is there, but the exact nature of the demand is still vague, as strategists try to come to terms with the nature of the new war, and the new enemy.

To figure out what the future holds for the development and procurement of new weaponry from the American military hardware producers, we need to examine the nature of post-Cold War trends in the defense industry. The legacy of the Reagan years was prevalent during the 1980s where many companies, which had previously maintained a significant client base in the civilian marketplace, were lured over to becoming exclusively defense contractors. A prime example is Bath Iron Works, one of two US shipyards who build destroyers for the US Navy. Before the boom in defense spending in the early and mid-1980s, the company was split equally between civilian and military contracts. It switched over to exclusively building warships for the Navy. By the end of the decade, the shipbuilders at Bath and other yards were virtually cut-off from the civilian market, and were so specialized that any return to supplying something other than ships or weapons platforms would entail a complete restructuring of the yard and its work force. These were golden years for these companies; in 1985 alone the US military spent $5.8 billion on warships, which was roughly half its expenditure on military aircraft during the same fiscal year. Missiles and ordnance spending was collectively in excess of $5 billion, while over $1 billion alone was spent on buying new tanks for the army. With post-Cold War hindsight, it seems obvious this level of military expenditure was not going to last forever, but this was not so clear at the time. When weapons procurement was at an all-time high, so too was the level of spending on research into new weapons

LEFT: A Tactical Electronic Warfare Squadron 140 (VAQ-140) EA-6B Prowler aircraft is shown over the nuclear-powered aircraft carrier USS *Dwight D Eisenhower.* Carrier Air Wing 7 is assigned to the *Eisenhower.*

ABOVE: Sailors and aircrew attached to Light Helicopter Antisubmarine Squadron 47 conduct hot-in-flight refueling of a SH-60B Seahawk helicopter from the deck of the USS *Antietam*. Hot-in-flight refueling is necessary when landing to refuel on a smaller US Navy vessel would be too dangerous.

LEFT: A Navy CH-46 Sea Knight helicopter delivers another pallet of bombs to the flight deck of the USS *John F Kennedy*.

ABOVE, RIGHT: A final inspection is made of the firing pins of 500lb bombs mounted underneath an F-14 Tomcat on the flight deck of the USS *Dwight D Eisenhower*.

RIGHT: A Tomcat launches from the the USS *Enterprise* and behind a Hawkeye maneuvers into position.

RIGHT: The frigate USS *Doyle* cruises the Caribbean Sea on its way to Colombia, South America

BELOW: USS *Kitty Hawk* tests the newly-installed Rolling Airframe Missile (RAM). RAM is a lightweight, quick-reaction, high-firepower anti-ship weapon system, designed as an all-weather, low-cost, self-defense system against anti-ship missiles.

systems. Many companies were allocated research and development (R&D) funding direct from the government. In the aerospace industry for example, $20 million, 80 percent of its research funding, came from the government in 1985, which was equivalent to over half of the full government R&D allocation to the private sector. For the military, this was an efficient way to encourage new weapons and technology research; paying private contractors to do the work for them. When the federal government cut the defense budget, not only defense contractors and jobs were hit, but weapons research also suffered.

The end of the Cold War was not the only impetus for change. Increasing concern about the public sector deficit led to calls for a cutback in military expenditure, and in 1987 the defense budget (and more importantly its consequent spending on weaponry) fell in real terms for the first time in a decade. The end of the Cold War four years later meant that the incoming Clinton administration would be able to continue this cutback in government spending on weapons procurement, electing to spend the money on the budget deficit rather than on new (and increasingly redundant) tanks, guns, and aircraft. While the effect of defense cuts on the dependent contractors was clearly understood, the government was largely powerless to help, as

ABOVE: Ground crew at the US Naval Air Station, Patuxent River, MD, load an AGM-65E Maverick onto a wing station of a US Marine Corps AV-8B Harrier 2.

RIGHT: The laser-guided Maverick air-to-ground missile is shown scoring a direct hit on an M53 tracked gun target at Eglin Air Force Base, Florida.

Congress vetoed a restructuring package which would have helped steer many of these defense contractors back into the civilian marketplace.

During the 1990s, there was a retrenchment in US military spending in general, and a reduction in weapons procurement and R&D in particular. The industry had not been hit so hard since the mid-1970s, during the immediate aftermath of the Vietnam War, when a similar number of companies had become dependent on military weapons contracts. Some two to three years after the end of the Cold War defense peak, the cutbacks in spending were reflected in the job market, although overseas exports provided a temporary respite through post-Gulf War arms sales. While cutbacks in America's armed forces resulted in a 25 percent reduction in military personnel between 1991 and 2001, the work

ABOVE: A B-2 Spirit approaches a KC-10A from the McGuire Air Force Base, New Jersey, during a training exercise. The B-2 Spirit is a multi-role bomber capable of delivering both conventional and nuclear munitions.

force in the defense industry was cut by a third. The boom of the 1980s, followed by the bust of the 1990s has left the industry in crisis, and has meant that many of America's leading defense contractors have been forced to restructure, and to look elsewhere for contracts. The biggest weapons-producing companies were those in the military aerospace industry, and they responded to the procurement crisis in four different ways. Some, such as General Dynamics and McDonnell Douglas, closed down a few of their less lucrative systems, and concentrated instead on those they did best, or knew would become the mainstays of the US military in the future. Others, such as Honeywell, removed themselves from the market, turning their defense divisions into stand-alone companies. Yet others merged, encouraged (and in some part-funded) by the US government. The Lockheed/Martin/Loral merger created a defense giant, capable of pooling its resources for weapons research, and ensuring better marketing connections in the Pentagon, and leverage with the US military's procurement offices. The final group (including Boeing and Rockwell) expanded their existing civilian arm, and downsized their weapons divisions. These big companies were able to weather the crisis for the most part because they could adopt the ideal balance between diversification and downsizing. For many smaller defense contractors, the options were less appealing. Many of these smaller companies (producing individual weapons systems or electronics) were forced to cut their production and staffing by as much as 50 percent. Others entered new commercial markets, or else expanded their marketing to overseas clients, making up in part for the reduced procurement levels by the US military.

During this crucial decade (1991–2001), the Pentagon was able to offer little in the way of guidance to the US defense contractors who supplied the military with weapons. Wall Street took the lead by encouraging mergers, diversification, and downsizing. Under the Clinton administration an attempt was made to provide some form of guidance for the weapons manufacturers. The Office of Economic Security was charged with researching the future relationship between the military and the defense industries, and to help both parties chart out a policy for the future. Nothing coherent emerged, as the Pentagon took the initiative by canceling several existing weapons research and production contracts,

ABOVE: F-16 "Wild Weasel" aircraft from the 35th Fighter Squadron., Misawa Air Base, fly a training mission over the Japanese coast.

in order to focus its dwindling resources on other areas. The result was more job losses in some areas, but increased levels of weapons procurement spending in others. For example, in 1999, United Technologies laid off 1,700 workers at its engine-making subsidiary, Pratt & Whitney. At the same time, Boeing, General Dynamics, and Northrop Grumman all benefited from increased investment in projects such the B-2 Stealth Bomber. The primary contractor for the B-2 is the Northrop Grumman Corporation, but Boeing, General Electric, and CTV were all major players in the project, and shared in the boost to their revenue and standing when new aircraft were ordered. In 2000, President Clinton's Defense Secretary William Cohen met with the Chief Executive Officers of the largest weapons corporations. He discussed ways the Pentagon could offer aid to the ailing defense industry. It was at this stage that two watershed policy changes were made. The first was from the Pentagon, which after a decade finally produced a coherent analysis of its future weapons needs for the coming century. This was based on an increased level of commitment to peacekeeping and humanitarian missions, the streamlining of the US military to work more effectively in non-conventional battlegrounds, and a decrease in the weapons of conventional warfare, such as

BELOW: A-10s were designed specially for the close air support mission and had the ability to combine large military loads and wide combat radius, which proved to be vital assets to America and its allies during Operation Desert Storm.

ABOVE: A US Air Force E-3 Sentry airborne warning and control system (AWACS) aircraft touches down at 4 Wing Cold Lake, Canada.

LEFT: A member of the USAF 51st Security Forces Squadron talks through his MCU-2P chemical/ biological mask as he communicates with other team members via radio while conducting a search.

ABOVE, RIGHT: A paratrooper from the US Army's 2nd Battalion, 1st Special Forces Group, jumps from a C-130 Hercules.

RIGHT: Clouds of dust billow out from behind a USAF C-17 Globemaster III as it lands on the dry lake bed of Bicycle Lake at Fort Irwin, California.

RIGHT and BELOW: During World War II the US Marine Corps proved itself the best amphibious force in the world, and since then it has become the United States' main "Force in Readiness," prepared to respond immediately to international crises. Among its large and potent inventory of arms is the LAV-25 (LAV—light armored vehicle) a wheeled vehicle that comes in a variety of forms including a TOW-armed antitank version (see page 31), a mortar carrier, a command and control vehicle, and as here, armed with a 0.79-in (20-mm) cannon.

ABOVE: The LAV-25 antitank variant is armed with the TOW missile.

antisubmarine destroyers, main battle tanks (MBTs), or state-of-the-art fighter aircraft. The second change was in the field of weapons procurement. As part of the reforms introduced by President Clinton's government, procurement reforms were introduced, aimed at eliminating unnecessary or wasteful military specifications, a tactic which many defense contractors argued was a ploy designed to favor the "chosen" defense companies. It was hoped that by changing the specifications when new systems were tendered, the industries who had diversified away from purely military markets might be able to reap the benefits as well as the main players in the industry. While this opened the marketplace to more competition and lowered procurement costs, it did little to help the industry as a whole, although it made the Pentagon reexamine its procedures.

The whole system of weapons research and procurement was a thorny issue during the late 1990s. Well-publicized examples of sheer incompetence in military procurement, such as the M2 Bradley AFV, clearly cost the American taxpayers billions of dollars through changes in specifications, the use of unsuitable components, and through the suppliers charging what they thought the market could bear for their product. Claims that the US Army spent $1,500 on a toilet roll holder were often exaggerated, but these "urban myths" also had a basis in fact. Weapons research projects are either allocated to the defense industry, who are tasked with developing proposals, or conducted by the US military. Government research departments such as the US Army Research Laboratory work up their own plans for weapons or weapons systems, then invite appropriate defense contractors to tender for production of the new system. In the past it was considered more efficient to allow the contractors themselves to conduct much of this research, as they were able to adapt the specifications to suit their own weapons manufacturing facilities and production systems. Spiraling costs and intense political scrutiny of research and development methods have led to a cutback in government sponsored weapons research in the private sector, and instead the Pentagon is trying to increase the use of its own in-house weapons development organizations. The Department of Defense is in overall charge of all weapons research programs, and is now instituting a streamlined and fairer method of tendering for production and procurement. Given the long lead

time in weapons research and production, wher*e a weapons system might take a decade or more from initial concept to production, the whole defense industry will still be acclimatizing to these changes for another decade. Military planners consequently have to work in 15-year cycles. It is expected that by 2015, the new kinds of weapons systems, developed and experimented before the start of the war on terrorism, will be in full-scale production; the perfect weapons for an old kind of war. This lag in production and procurement means that the US military has to make do with whatever weapons it has available to fight its new war.

Long-term planning and procurement is by necessity out of date. The Pentagon needs to make a best-possible estimate of the pace of technology, the future role of the US military, and the budget it can expect to receive a decade from now. The current military strategic plan produced during the administration of President Clinton was inherited by President Bush, and although it took into account the expected pace of technological change, it was unable to predict the aftermath of September 11, 2001. Under these existing plans, the annual cost to the Department of Defense to replace its existing arsenal of weapons systems with next-generation weapons or even to replace existing systems in a one-for-one exchange has all been regulated. In 2002–3, $65 billion was set aside for procurement, a sum which was expected to rise to $95 billion in 2015–16. In October 2001, as part of the new commitment to the war on terrorism, an additional $15 billion was made available for new weaponry. In other words, over the next decade, the American defense industry can expect another boom period, just like it enjoyed during the Vietnam War, or during the administration of President Reagan.

One problem with this is that it is far from clear that all of the new next-generation weapon systems called for under the current plan are necessary in this new style of war. The Department of Defense is therefore considering scaling back on new systems, and instead buying larger quantities of current-generation systems (such as F-16Cs or A10As), rather than their high-tech successors. By reducing procurement costs in this way, more money can be channeled to fund changes in the military structures necessary to fight the war on terrorism. This suggestion has met with criticism, as some analysts believe that the budget needed to keep the US military adequately equipped with modern weaponry over the long term is inadequate.

Although research and development teams, military analysts, weapons manufacturers, and politicians all have a say in the commissioning of new weapons systems, recent changes mean that it is difficult to predict future needs. Given the low level of technology expected in the war on terrorism, aging weapons systems such as the venerable B-52 bomber might still have a place in the US Air Force a decade from now. The drawback is that as weapons systems, planes, and warships get older, maintenance costs spiral, and maintenance times get longer. Although next-generation weapons systems may be a preferable option for the future, the large financial commitment needed for their production may not be the best possible use of resources.

The Pentagon is busy trying to work out the ramifications of its first war of the 21st century for its long-term plans. It is highly likely that this fresh look at procurement, planning, and development might force a new approach to planned modernization in the future. In particular, these trends might call into question the current plan for replacing the US military's already large and effective fleet of large surface warships and tanks with costly next-generation systems. Instead, it might make sense to devote greater resources to weapons which are better suited to the new style of warfare. These might include more cruise missile firing warships, converting the SSBN fleet to become Tomahawk platforms, developing "extended-range precision artillery systems" such as the Army Tactical Missile System (ATACMS), or it might even mean concentrating on building more long-range bombers and unmanned combat air vehicles (UCAVs). Until the Pentagon decides what weapons it needs to fulfill its new mission, the soldiers, sailors and airmen of the US military will have to make the best use they can of the weapons they already have.

LEFT: The Hawk surface-to-air missile entered service in the 1960s and since then has been upgraded by the MIM-23B Improved Hawk. It was intended that the Patriot would replace it but the Hawk still continues in service.

Weaponry Developments in the Armed Forces since the Cold War

The US Army

The end of the Cold War caught the army largely unawares. Plans were laid to "downsize," but the army, which had been developed to fight the Soviet Union in Germany, had one last moment of mechanized glory. In the Gulf War (1991), the US Army deployed armored and mechanized infantry formations;.M1A1 Abrams tanks, Bradley APCs, plus the full supporting weaponry associated with armored or mechanized warfare. The weaponry deployed by the army during the campaign ensured that the Iraqis were outclassed and outfought. Following an initial overwhelming artillery bombardment that largely broke the will of the enemy front-line formations, the superior weaponry of the American army ensured that victory was swift and complete. The Iraqis were cooperative in that they passively awaited their fate, a bit like a sacrificial lamb to the slaughter. Following the Gulf War and the shift in emphasis to an interventionist military role, it became clear that not all opponents or battlegrounds would present the army with such a golden opportunity to demonstrate its might. It also provided the military and the American public with a false expectation of what a future conflict might entail. Losses were extremely light, but in a war against a more determined enemy, fighting on ground of his own choosing, then the casualty list would be much higher.

This was amply demonstrated on October 3, 1993 during an operation by Task Force Rangers in Mogadishu, Somalia. An operation to apprehend known Somali warlords in downtown Mogadishu ended in disaster, despite the presence of US Rangers and specially trained operatives from the secret Delta Force. The attack was designed to be a quick insertion, then extraction, and the soldiers were covered by MH-60K Blackhawk gunships, AH-6J Little Bird attack helicopters, and transport versions of both helicopters (MH-60K and MH-6).

RIGHT: The AH-64 Apache is armed with the Hellfire antitank missile whose guidance system is being upgraded with the Longbow targeting system.

LEFT and BELOW: The "Black Hawk Down" episode in Somalia showed that the US Army needed to keep a flexible light – as opposed to mechanized – infantry force such as that provided by the Rangers and the 10th Mountain Division. Armored vehicles and mechanized warfare are essential for operations like "Desert Storm" or to fight the on NATO's Central Front, but the threats of the new millennium require more flexibility.

When two Blackhawk helicopters were shot down, the situation deteriorated, as the troops were required to extend their perimeter to encompass the two crash sites, in the face of growing and heavy Somali opposition. Faced with a city population where almost everyone carried an AK-47, casualties were inevitable. What followed was the virtual siege of the insertion team, and heavy casualties on both sides. The lack of available AC-130H Specter gunships meant that fire support was limited, so the Rangers had to be rescued the hard way, by ground troops. The 2nd Battalion of the 14th Infantry Regiment (nicknamed "The Dragons") was a "light infantry" outfit, part of the 10th Mountain Division. Tasked with the rescue mission, the battalion drove Humvees armed with 1.6in (40mm) Mk. 19 automatic grenade launchers escorting sandbagged trucks. Helicopter gunships and elements of other UN peacekeeping outfits provided support. They fought their way through the Somali city, rescued the Rangers and Delta teams, and managed to extricate themselves without major loss after a bitter running firefight lasting several hours.

The total human cost of the operation for the Rangers was 11 dead, five missing (presumed dead), one captured, and 60 wounded, while two of their

rescuers were killed and 26 wounded. Somali casualties have been placed at 1,126, including 312 dead. This bloodbath caused a sensation in America, as the photographs of dead soldiers and aircrew being dragged through the streets by a hostile crowd was not what the American public had come to expect from a supposed relief mission and peacekeeping effort. The operation brought an end to American involvement in the region, and a reevaluation of the role of the US military in future overseas ventures.

If one positive development emerged from the "Black Hawk Down" fiasco, it was the demonstration that well-trained American "light infantry" were a useful part of the Army's reactive force. The Army lists the tasks expected of an infantry battalion, and during the operation in Mogadishu, "The Dragons" performed 23 of the 60 on the list, including "breach of defended obstacles, bypass of enemy forces, fighting a meeting engagement, attack of a built-up area, and withdrawal under pressure. During the last decade of the Cold War, American military planners had seriously thought of converting all non-airborne or Ranger infantry formations into mechanized infantry. This was a reaction to the build-up of Soviet mechanized forces in Germany, but following the

ABOVE: The M1 Abrams performed brilliantly in the Gulf War and its armor protection was so efficient that Iraqi T-72 shells simply bounced off.

BELOW: The TOW-armed Bradley also performed with distinction in the Gulf War: the weapon system allowed US forces to keep up the pace of armored thrusts.

LEFT: The M113 has two mortar-carrier versions—the M125 with an 3-in (81-mm) mortar and the M106 with a 4.2 in(107mm).

BELOW, LEFT and RIGHT: Realistic training is essential if troops are to perform their jobs in combat. The "Dragons" in Somalia performed 23 of the 60 tasks expected of an infantry battalion and rescued the Ranger and Delta force operatives in the face of massive numbers of armed but untrained Somalis.

RIGHT: The M47 Dragon antitank missile also proved particularly useful as a bunker-buster in the Gulf War.

BELOW: Many of the Military Occupation Specialities require the ability to use sophisticated technology in a combat environment.

ABOVE: A big advantage for the Army would be having superior night vision and sighting equipment.. This would make target acquisition easier to quantify.

end of the Cold War, these mechanized units were no longer of much use. As one wag put it, the army was perfectly structured for fighting the German Army in 1944–45 by the end of the Cold War. Fortunately it also retained a number of "leg-infantry" units such as the 10th Mountain Division, and these formations were given a disproportionate level of involvement in the decade following the Gulf War, as peacekeepers, interventionists, and humanitarian providers.

The new commitment of the Army to the war on terrorism caught them wrong-footed, as they were still adjusting themselves to a post-Cold War strength, and were in the middle of a reconsideration of their role and mode of operation. During the years following the American withdrawal from Somalia the Army was called upon to operate in the Balkans, and was even readying itself to fight a conventional war in Kosovo. Given the lack of effectiveness of heavy armor and mechanized units, the army necessarily relied on its "light infantry" formations, its Rangers, and its airborne troops. The success of the Kosovo campaign through airpower provided another false impression; that wars could be won without putting troops on the ground. This myth was dispelled in Afghanistan. As one American colonel put it; "They have yet to make a jet fighter-bomber with a bayonet stud." Further involvement in the war on terrorism also means that both the Army and the public have to be prepared for toe-to-toe fighting with often determined and well-trained opponents, and casualties are inevitable.

Since Korea and Vietnam, the public has become unused to high casualty rates, and consequently the avoidance of casualties has become a cornerstone of "peacetime" American doctrine. This will inevitably change. In an age when other branches of the American military are becoming increasingly reliant on high-tech weaponry, the US Army is finding that the "grunt" on the ground with his rifle is the most important weapon in its arsenal.

The US Navy and US Marine Corps

Warships and the nature of naval warfare have changed radically since the end of World War II, a series of technical developments which was second only to the introduction of the ironclad in its far-reaching effect on seapower. The development of nuclear submarines, new forms of antisubmarine warfare, antiaircraft, and antiship missile systems, along with the revolution in electronic warfare and command and control, evolved during the half century between 1945 and the end of the Cold War. Two new capital ships evolved during this period. The nuclear ballistic missile submarine (SSBN), formed an arm of the Navy which served no function apart from being a covert launching platform for a weapon of mass destruction (WMD); a nuclear missile. As such it was not strictly a naval weapons system, and following the end of the Cold War the SSBN fleet lacked a clear role as the United States was forced to evaluate the effectiveness of its WMD arsenal. The second capital ship of the late 20th century (and the early 21st) is the supercarrier, a weapons platform whose role has changed with relative ease from the Cold War to the post-Cold War world. The aircraft carrier emerged from World War II as the preeminent warship type of the conflict, and this importance has continued into the 21st century. Another ship type to emerge from the Pacific War was the amphibious assault ship, and its subsequent development has increased the versatility and effectiveness of the US Marine Corps. Today, a combination of naval air-power and marine deployment capability has created a naval force which is well suited to the new demands of the new century, and together they form the backbone of America's rapid reaction capability.

As for warships as weapons platforms, the late 20th century saw a dramatic transformation, from the gun-armed warship to the guided-missile platform. Ships are often referred to as "platforms," as their effectiveness is largely measured by the weapons and control systems with which they are fitted. The old divisions of warships by type (i.e. cruiser, destroyer, frigate etc.) have no longer the same meaning as they did a half-century ago, and their definitions have become blurred. The main elements of this naval revolution have been as much in the fields of electronics and command and control as in weapons. Indeed, all three elements are necessarily combined into a modern naval "weapons system," as a package. Much of these systems are hidden, taking the form of computers, or centralized data-handling systems, such as those found in a US Navy warship's

BELOW: The guided missile destroyer USS *Mitscher* heads out to sea this morning from the channel at Port Everglades, Florida., after a three-day port visit to Fort Lauderdale.

combat information center (CIC) or action information center (AIC). At the height of the Cold War, the US Navy had some of the most efficient weapons control and ship command systems in the world.

Naval warfare has largely become a matter of data management, where special "flagship" vessels were capable of performing complex tasks. A single warship is now capable of analyzing data from its own systems and those of other warships or merchant vessels in its task group. This information could then be redirected to the appropriate weapons system on any of the ships, and the appropriate action taken, whether it be firing an antimissile barrage or computing the data for a shore bombardment. Following the end of the Cold War, the need for these "flagship systems" remains, as was demonstrated during the Gulf War when US task force commanders were able to plan then coordinate strikes by naval guns, cruise missiles, and naval aircraft, all from one CIC. Another important development over the last decade was the degree with which local commanders (or "deployed commanders" as the Navy calls them), can consult with their superiors virtually instantaneously. This means that political decision-makers, task-force commanders, and the Naval staff in the Pentagon can all react to events as they unfold, and dictate the appropriate level of response. This communications revolution means that a phenomenal

ABOVE: At sea with the USS *Essex* Amphibious Readiness Group (ARG) in 2002. The ARG provides a flexible and quick reacting Navy-Marine Corps team.

LEFT: The ARG from the USS *Essex* practice formation steaming during the semi-annual amphibious integration training exercise known as Blue-Green Workups..

RIGHT: During a training exercise, two Navy Special Warfare Rigid-Hull Inflatable Boats (NSW RHIBs) are launched from the amphibious transport dock ship USS *Shreveport* to pick up SEAL team members.

BELOW: USS *John Paul Jones* leads a formation of ships in a series of close ship maneuvers.

BOTTOM: USS *Carl Vinson* launches a "Sea Sparrow" during a missile launch exercise as the ship was sailing toward Hawaii. A "Sea Sparrow" is a surface-to-air anti-missile defense system.

degree of naval firepower and naval airpower can be unleashed against an enemy target within seconds of the order being passed down from the President of the United States to his military advisors.

An example of the effectiveness of this sophisticated command and control system is provided by the employment of Tomahawk antiship missiles during the Gulf War and in Afghanistan. The Tomahawk was a weapon which was largely designed to counter Cold War enemy naval units in the European theater, and was adapted from a missile airframe which was already being developed to attack land-based targets. As a result the new weapon had a dual function, although the US Navy primarily relied on its nuclear attack submarine fleet and its naval aviation units to attack enemy surface task forces.

The missile had an over-the-horizon capability, so the control systems of the launching warship had to coordinate targeting information from satellites, surveillance aircraft, and shore positions to form an over-the-horizon-targeting (OTH-T) solution. This information was passed to a Fleet Command Center, where information was relayed to both the firing ship and the Pentagon. On the ship itself, an OTH-T system took the information, processed it, and readied the missile for launch. Once the Tomahawk was fired, its progress could be monitored, and a second strike

LEFT: The Aegis cruiser USS *Shiloh* fires an RGM-84A Harpoon missile during exercises, while the Spruance-class destroyer USS *Fletcher* awaits her turn to shoot.

BELOW, LEFT: The guided missile cruiser USS *Yorktown* fires her Mark 45, 5-inch, 54-caliber lightweight gun at a target drone during a gunnery exercise.

BOTTOM, LEFT: A standard missile leaves a trail of smoke as it is launched from the starboard side of USS *Vandegrift* and heads on an intercept course with an incoming "hostile" drone.

RIGHT: An F-14 Tomcat catches the wire on the flight deck of USS *Nimitz* during the first day of flight operations after the ship's 36-month refueling.

BELOW, RIGHT: An F/A-18 Hornet, piloted by US Air Force Major Philip Malebranche, from Virginia Beach, Virginia., is launched from the flight deck of USS *George Washington*

BOTTOM, RIGHT: A flight deck director hands off control of a Marine Corps AV-8B Harrier to another director after the aircraft touches down on the deck of the amphibious assault ship USS *Bataan*.

authorized from the highest level within seconds. This was the method used to target Tomahawk strikes during the attack on Al Qaida bases in Afghanistan in 2001–2; the strikes were launched from US Naval units in the Persian Gulf. The result was a weapon which extended the range and accuracy of naval power far beyond the conventional sphere of naval operations.

In a similar fashion, post-Cold War developments have stressed the value of maintaining air and amphibious assets in a constant state of readiness in the Middle East, and off other potential areas of conflict. Tomahawk missiles, for example, can strike targets far inland, and the supercarriers of the US Navy can launch strikes or fight for local air supremacy at considerable distances from their bases. Under this protective umbrella, US Marine Corps personnel can then be deployed virtually anywhere and at short notice, as they lack the cumbersome logistical and mechanical "tail" of most other troop types.

Although in the post-Cold War era the need for nuclear attack submarines or antisubmarine vessels has diminished, the striking power of the US Navy places it at the forefront of America's war on terrorism, as it gives the US government a tool which it can use with very little notice. Of all the three services, the Navy is the best suited to this new war, and to its new role.

ABOVE: A Standard Missile (SM-3) leaves the vertical launch system (VLS) of the cruiser USS *Lake Erie* during a combined Missile Defense Agency and US Navy flight test.

LEFT: Aviation ordnanceman, 2nd class, Alejandro Montalvo of Mocha, Puerto Rico, and aviation ordnanceman, 3rd class, Chris Tucker of Ocala, Florida, prepare a 2000 pound, MK-84 JDAM GPS guided weapon for loading on an F/A-18 Hornet on the flight deck of USS *George Washington*.

ABOVE: The USS *Normandy* fires its 5-in (127mm) guns at the training range on Vieques, Puerto Rico.

RIGHT: The USS *Greeneville* sits atop blocks in Dry Dock at the Pearl Harbor Naval Shipyard, Hawaii. The Los Angeles class attack submarine is dry-docked to assess damage and perform repairs.

FAR LEFT: US and Danish sailors watch as a crane lifts Mark 52 mines to the deck of the HDMS *Falster*.

LEFT: A US Navy diver attaches an inert satchel charge to a training mine.

RIGHT: The US Navy's Deep Submergence Rescue Vehicle Mystic (DSRV 1) is loaded aboard a USAF Reserve C-5A Galaxy aircraft.

The US Air Force

Like the Navy, the Air Force was designed to fight in a conventional war against the Soviet Union. To this end it developed sophisticated long-range strike aircraft, with complex arrays of electronics equipment, and a supporting fighter wing of the latest air supremacy aircraft. Experience gained during the Vietnam War proved invaluable in determining the best way to equip fighters for air-to-air combat missions, and in protecting strike aircraft with electronics. It also provided an impetus for the development of new types of munitions, particularly specialist antiradar, antirunway, and "bunker-buster" ordnance. These are useful in a conventional war but, together with the latest long-range air-to-air missiles (LRAMs), are less useful in the post-Cold War era.

The new role as a global policeman was one for which the Air Force was ill-prepared. In 1986, F-111s based in Britain bombed targets in Libya, in what might now be seen as an opening round in the war against terrorism. Operation "El-Dorado Canyon" was a relative success, as all five designated targets were hit, but the art of "surgical strikes" still had a long way to go, as civilian targets were also hit in the raid. This prompted further development of precision munition guidance systems. In December 1989, the United States launched "Operation Just Cause" when it invaded Panama, and the Air Force flew over 400 transport sorties with C-130, C-5, and C-141 transport aircraft, placing over 19,000 troops into the combat zone, together with their supplies and equipment. This was made possible by the seizure of Panama's International Airport by airborne forces, and Air Force gunships and helicopters covered the deployment. This operation was unusual in that a high-quality base was available to permit the full deployment of the Air Force's resources. This was not an option in most Third World or Eastern European countries.

RIGHT: Transitioning from trail into diamond formation, the number four slot pilot of the US Air Force Thunderbirds has a very unique perspective.

BELOW: An Air Force weapons loader from the 28th Air Expeditionary Wing prepares a 2000-pound bomb to be loaded into a B-1B Lancer bomber.

RIGHT: HH-60G *Pave Hawk* practices hoist procedures.

FAR RIGHT: An Air Force crew-chief replaces the brakes on a KC-10A Extender in support of Operation Enduring Freedom.

BELOW: The 20th Special Operations Squadron, located at Hurlburt Field, Florida, is one of eight flying squadrons within the 16th Special Operations Wing. Known as the "Green Hornets," the 20th SOS flies the MH-53J Pave Low IIIE, the Air Force's most sophisticated helicopter.

The Gulf War in 1991 came at a time when the Air Force had not yet been forced to implement the post-Cold War cutbacks ordered by the government. Consequently it was able to deploy substantial resources to the Middle East, as part of "Operation Desert Storm." F-15s, F-16s, F-111s, F-4Gs, transport aircraft, electronic warfare aircraft (EWs), and helicopter gunships all had a part to play in the conflict, and for probably the last time they were able to employ the full panoply of Cold War technology. By the time the war ended, Allied air forces had flown over 110,000 sorties, and had devastated the Iraqi army and air force—112 Iraqi aircraft were destroyed, a third in air-to-air combat. The technology employed by the US Air Force proved highly effective, and proved overwhelmingly superior to the weaponry arrayed against it in the form of surface-to-air missiles (SAMs), or aircraft weapons systems. The war also saw the deployment of the old and the new versions of American long-range strike aircraft. B-52 bombers flew 1,624 missions, and dropped 72,000 bombs on enemy targets. This cudgel was

ABOVE: A KC-10A from McGuire Air Force Base, New Jersey, refuels a B-2 Spirit during a training exercise.

augmented by the latest Lockheed F-117A Stealth fighters, which flew 1,300 sorties, and dropped 2,000 tons of bombs. For the Air Force, the war was personified by the deployment of precision bombing weapons. Infrared, laser-guided bombs launched from aircraft resulted in the virtual destruction of the Iraqi army during its retreat from Kuwait, augmented by even more lethal weapons.

The BLU-82 is a 15,000lb (680kg) free-fall, fuel-air bomb, nicknamed "Big Blue." Also known as "The Mother of all Bombs," the BLU-82 was the largest conventional bomb in the Air Force arsenal, and it was used to great effect during the war. It was found to be effective in clearing enemy minefields, and its use as a platform for "daisy-cutter" munitions and even as a "leaflet bomb" (containing millions of instructions on how Iraqi soldiers could surrender) proved that the Air Force could be innovative in its use of its weaponry. Most air-to-air victories of the US Air Force (35 out of 40) were attributed to F-15C Eagles of the 33d Tactical Fighter Wing, who employed radar-guided AIM-7 Sparrows and even old AIM-9 Sidewinders to shoot down their opponents. Even more Iraqi aircraft were destroyed on the ground than in the air, as precision bombing of airfields helped decimate the Iraqi ability to launch concerted air attacks on Allied forces.

In the ten years between the Gulf War and the commencement of the war on terrorism, the US Air Force became involved in both Africa and the Balkans, first as a supplier of humanitarian aid and as a peacekeeper, then as a combatant. This meant a change of emphasis, and in the Operations "Provide Relief," "Restore Hope," "Provide Promise" or "Provide Comfort," transport aircraft were at the forefront of the Air Force effort. Aircraft such as the C-130E proved capable of delivering food and medical supplies in significant quantities. During this period aircraft designed during the last days of the Cold War entered service, including the B-2A Spirit. Twenty-one of these aircraft have since been built, and while they were designed to carry a varied combination of weaponry – from iron or cluster bombs, nuclear payloads, and near-precision weapons – their most impressive feature is their range. The aircraft incorporates a low-observable (LO) Stealth structure

LEFT: Crew members from the two C-17 Globemaster III airlifters celebrate after returning to Ramstein Air Base, Germany, following a humanitarian airdrop mission over eastern Afghanistan.

BELOW: A B-52H Stratofortress from the 419th Flight Test Squadron from Edwards Air Force Base, California, releases a Joint Direct Attack Munition during a recent test.

LEFT: F-15s from the 114th Fighter Squadron, Kinglsey Field Air National Guard Base, Klamath Falls, Oregon, fly in formation over Craer Lake National Park.

BELOW: Working under nighttime red light, a boom operator shuts down the Pacer Craig navigational system aboard his KC-135.

BOTTOM: Airmen delivered tons of relief supplies, like the daily rations pictured, into poverty-stricken areas of Afghanistan as part of the humanitarian relief effort, Operation Enduring Freedom.

with an incredible aerodynamic design, and employs the latest technology in terms of electronics, navigation, and weapons control. At a time when the US Air Force is hindered by its lack of secure overseas bases close to trouble-spots, the employment of long-range transport aircraft such as the C-141 Starlifter and the C-130J allows it to fulfill its airlift mission from bases on American soil. The deployment of aircraft such as the B-2A takes this one step further, as recent events in Afghanistan have demonstrated. These Stealth bombers flew to Afghanistan from America, dropped their payload with precision, then flew back home. Aircraft have come a long way in the 20th century. The question is whether the US Air Force can maintain this momentum, and design aircraft suited to its new role in the war on terrorism. In order to deploy its full array of Cold War weaponry, it needs a conventional battlefield, or at least conventional targets. The ability of the Air Force to adapt during the Gulf War has still to be demonstrated as it "regears" for the first long-term war in American history. This war is also the first one since 1945 when control of the skies is less important than airborne surveillance, targeting, and the precision bombing of terrorist targets.

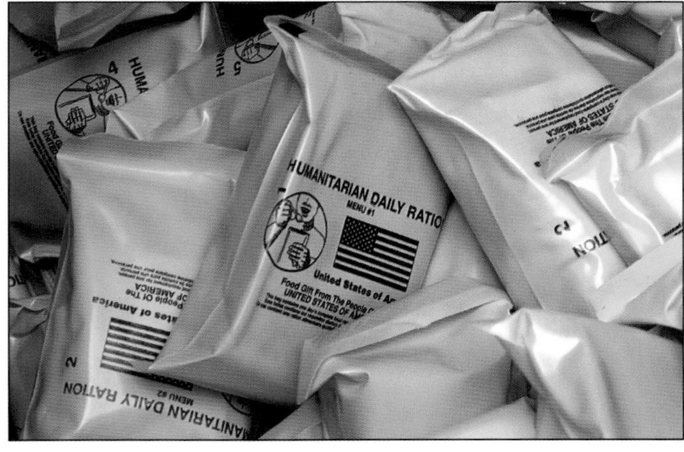

ABOVE: A B-1B from the 28th Bomb Wing at Ellsworth Air Force Base, South Dakota, flies over the pyramids in Egypt.

LEFT: MH-53J Pave Low IIIE flies a training mission near Kirtland Air Force Base, New Mexico. The MH-53J's mission is to perform low-level, long-range, undetected penetration into denied areas, day or night, in adverse weather.

ABOVE: The pilot banks his F-15D Eagle as he looks for opposition aircraft while flying a training mission over the Pacific Ocean near Japan.

RIGHT: A 33rd Rescue Squadron HH-60G takes off from the USS *Juneau* during ship landing training in the Pacific. The primary mission of the HH-60G Pave Hawk helicopter is to conduct day or night operations into hostile environments to recover downed aircrew or other isolated personnel during war. Because of its versatility, the HH-60G is also tasked to perform military operations other than war. These tasks include civil search and rescue, emergency aeromedical evacuation (MEDEVAC), disaster relief, international aid, counterdrug activities, and NASA space shuttle support.

LEFT: A USAF F-16CJ Fighting Falcon soars in the skies over Turkey before being refueled in flight.

BELOW: An A/OA-10 Thunderbolt II is refueled in flight by a KC-135R Stratotanker.

The Future Demands of the US Military

The war on terrorism has been a driving force for change within the US military. Even before the tragic events of September 11, 2001, Secretary of Defense Donald Rumsfeld forced the US Government of President George W Bush to confront the need for drastic changes in the way the US military is equipped, and in its perception of future roles. Since the Gulf War in 1991, several military flash-points have provided signposts to the future of American military involvement; Bosnia, Somalia, and Kosovo being the prime examples. During the decade between the wars in Kuwait and Afghanistan, American political leaders were primarily concerned with the opportunity for "downsizing" their national military machine following the end of the Cold War. This was achieved without reading the signs that the country's armed forces were looking increasingly ill-prepared for the new kind of war which they might be called upon to fight in. The consequence of this lack of direction from above was a growing disenchantment in military circles as servicemen were unable to understand their future role, even though many could see that changes were desperately needed. Secretary Rumsfeld began to address the problem in a series of discussion papers and directives, but the procedure of redirecting the US military to fight a new kind of war had only just started when the airplane hijackers struck on September 11, 2001.

The resulting campaign in Afghanistan came as a real shock to the US military, as it was called upon to launch an air and missile campaign against a distant country. They then had to introduce ground troops, far from the supporting air bases and supply depots which the army required to fulfil its mission, and to resupply or reequip its troops. Of all three services, the US Air Force and the US Army were least prepared to undertake this new role. Given the very nature of the environment in which they operate, the US Navy and the US Marines were better placed to transform themselves into tools to fight terrorist rather than the forces of another global superpower.

It was suddenly discovered that America's military arsenal was virtually obsolete, as it was largely unsuited to its new usage. For a decade the weapons supplied to the US military, as well as the military machine itself, had failed to evolve and it paid the price in its inability to react quickly and efficiently to counter the new threat of global terrorism. The Gulf War was not the war of the future, as many military

BELOW: The aircraft carrier USS *John C. Stennis* executes a sharp turn to starboard.

LEFT: A camouflaged LAV-R tank rolls through the desert, blowing up a cloud of sand behind it.

BELOW: Modern US military doctrine emphasizes speed of reaction and the US Marine Corps plays a significant role in this approach. It is able to land forces by sea or air and support them with its organic air-power. Photo shows a USMC LAV on exercise.

strategists and weapons contractors had imagined. It was probably the last of the great combined tank, infantry, and airpower campaigns fought on a scale reminiscent of World War II, using conventional albeit high-tech weapons. The war was characterized by the massed deployment of heavy M1 Abrams tanks, attack helicopters (such as the Apache), and tank-busting aircraft such as the A-10 Groundhog. Airborne divisions leap-frogged across the battlefield by helicopter, warships provided naval gunfire support, and UN aircraft flew ground-attack sorties which tore up the Iraqi front-line defenses and reserve echelons. The set-piece attack was what the American military had been preparing for since the end of World War II, expect the opponent they had always envisaged was the Soviet Union, and the expected battleground was Central Europe, not the Middle East. This huge military force took time to deploy, and although it was well suited to the relatively open deserts of Kuwait, it was a military cudgel which was as unsubtle as it was obsolete.

The new role of the US military emphasizes speed of reaction and the ability to strike without waiting to build up a huge logistical support base. It means deploying light, well-equipped forces, and supporting

ABOVE: Crew members of the USS *Thomas Gates* stand by at their replenishment station as the ship makes its approach on the USS *Kalamazoo* for underway refueling off the coast of Florida.

LEFT: A Petty Officer uses a sextant to plot the navigational position of the USS *Abraham Lincoln* on route to the Persian Gulf on a routine six-month deployment.

LEFT: An F/A-18 Hornet is directed by a yellow shirt to the forward port catapult on the flight deck of the USS *Enterprise* as the ship conducts flight operations in the Mediterranean Sea.

BELOW: The USS *Kitty Hawk* sits pier side in Apra Harbor, Guam on a routine deployment en route to the Arabian Gulf.

them with airpower and naval gunfire or missile strikes if required. Events in Afghanistan and the Middle East indicate that the US military cannot rely on the use of the airbases and supply infrastructures of other friendly powers, but have to be prepared to fight alone, and far from home. Fortunately the United States of America already has the forces at hand to fulfil this new mission.

The US Navy are the only branch of the US armed services capable of reacting to these new demands, through the deployment of aircraft carrier and amphibious warfare groups. The deployment of US Marines, the use of carrier-based strike aircraft, and the use of naval gunfire support, or ship or submarine-launched cruise missiles are all vital parts of the naval arsenal. Apart from naval gunnery, all of these elements or weapons have been used to great effect in Afghanistan. However, to give them credit, the US Air Force, as well as naval aviation elements of the US Navy, responded to the attack on the World Trade Center and the Pentagon. They provided Combat Air Patrols (CAPs) along borders of the United States, and around its major cities and military installations.

The sight of F-16s or F-18s patrolling the skies of New York, Washington, and Philadelphia must have provided the inhabitants of these cities some modicum of relief. In addition, both services provide radar and antiaircraft protection from ships and aircraft operating along the Atlantic and Pacific seaboards. In particular, AEGIS-equipped cruisers and destroyers were stationed off Long Island and in the Chesapeake Bay, protecting New York City, Washington DC, and Norfolk, Virginia.

Of all the arms of the military, the Army has the biggest changes to make. Since the end of the Cold War and the Gulf War which followed, the US Army has retained its armored and mechanized formations, which need a large logistical tail, as well as supply bases and time for military preparation. There are

BELOW: Realistic training is essential to prepare US troops for all types of future engagements.

ABOVE and RIGHT: It doesn't matter how heavy the firepower is, it has to be accurate. Training on the ranges and in combat conditions is essential particularly for light infantry forces that rely on their small arms rather than heavy mechanized weaponry.

very few "leg infantry" or light infantry formations available for deployment, and when the decision was made to enter Afghanistan, only the 10th Mountain Division was available for deployment. These light formations rely on infantry firepower, and often highly sophisticated personal or support weapons, but they have the advantage that for all intents, they can be loaded onto a plane, and flown into a trouble-spot. The weakness of these troops, including the Airborne formations (the 101st and 82nd Airborne Divisions) and even the US Rangers is that they need to be flown from established bases.

If friendly powers are reluctant to grant the US military permission to use their bases close to the trouble-spot, or even if they refuse to let them travel through their airspace, then the deployment range of these troops is limited. To transport combat troops in

ABOVE: Two Blackhawks and a Chinook touch down. These new types of helicopter have begun to supercede the older models.

a fleet of transport aircraft such as the Galaxy, the receiving airbase needs to be able to take the huge quantities of planes, stores, and men which are involved in such a deployment. This means that somebody has to secure the base first, and in most cases, to adapt it to take large transport aircraft. While it was envisaged that these troops would be flown into bases in Europe, this was not a major problem. As the US Army now faces the likelihood that it could be called upon to insert troops into Third World countries, or ones lacking substantial airbases, then it needs to reevaluate its method of transportation, and more importantly, the equipping of its troops.

The nature of the new war is something that requires more than military hardware. It needs resolve, and the US commitment to the conflict has demonstrated that at least for the moment, that resolution is shared by both the American public, the government and the military. For the first time in its history, the United States is opposed by an enemy, who if it could detonate a bomb which would kill every last American would do so with glee. This hatred is not directed at Americans as individuals, but as a nation; a symbol of a corrupt, immoral, and Godless state, preying on the weaknesses of the Third World in general and on Islam in particular. The antagonism of people who hold this viewpoint is exacerbated by the increasing religious fervor encompassing much of the Muslim world, and the involvement of the United States in combating terrorism. In a world filled with weapons of mass destruction, suicide bombers, and religious zealots, the United States is locked into a war involving diplomacy, reason, and intelligence gathering as much as in the deployment of America's formidable arsenal. It is not a clash between civilizations, only one between civilized people and extremists intent on their destruction. These terrorists want to turn it into a war between East and West, Islam and

Christianity, tolerance and barbarism. America is at war, and its leaders, commanders, and above all its public, need to address some difficult issues concerning the waging of this war on terror. In war, you kill your enemies until they stop fighting you. This is particularly true here, as the hard-core terrorists who are waging war against America will not quit while they are alive. In the attack on Afghanistan, innocent civilians were killed.

The fearsome arsenal available to the United States far exceeds that which flattened the cities of Germany in World War II. In that conflict, civilian casualties were inevitable, as they will be in any future campaign in the war on terrorism. The

TOP: M-60 gun. Despite modern advances in weaponry, simple and robust infantry support weapons are still highly effective.

RIGHT: The camouflaged sniper is still frequently used, to deadly effect.

RIGHT: A Petty Officer checks a pump's status on the Auxiliary Engineering Officer of the Watch Central Control Station aboard the Navy's first "Smart Ship," USS *Yorktown*.

FAR RIGHT, TOP: Four A-10A Thunderbolts shimmer in the desert heat waves as they taxi out for a combat patrol.

FAR RIGHT, BOTTOM: A 355th Fighter Squadron A/AO-10 Thunderbolt II moves into position for refueling.

difference is, today the use of less indiscriminate weapons provides military planners with the opportunity to reduce civilian casualties to a minimum. The use of precision guided weapons allow the USA to launch devastating raids at specific targets. This technology will come into its own in the coming decade, but there is still a place in the military toolbox for the sledgehammer as well as the lightsaber.

From the beginning of the conflict in Afghanistan, American service personnel were embroiled in close-combat fighting in caves reminiscent of the struggles on the Pacific atolls during World War II. War is a dehumanizing and horrific experience, and despite all the technological advantages enjoyed by America's servicemen, war can still come down to brutal close-quarters contests; grenades, rifles, knives, and bayonets. As an American Lieutenant said on Pork Chop Hill during the Korean War, "Bayonets ... right out of the Stone Age! Where's all this push-button warfare we've been hearing about?" His companion, another Lieutenant, wryly commented in reply, "We're the push-buttons."

This book explores the tools which make up the arsenal of today's US military machine; its aircraft, warships, guns, artillery, missiles, munitions, and rockets. Many of them will stand or fall as weapons systems by their performance in battle. All the B-2

Stealth Bombers, Tomahawk missiles, or AEGIS missile cruisers in the world can't flush out terrorists from a mountain cave complex in Afghanistan. A well-led, well-motivated, and well-trained United States Marine armed with an assault rifle and bayonet is still the best tool for the job, just as he was at Mount Suribachi on Iwo Jima, or the Citadel in Hue City, or the Legation Compound in Peking. Somehow, for all the technology in the world, for all the vast firepower at the beck and call of an American commander in the field or at sea, it often all comes down to a scared young grunt with a rifle.

AIR WEAPONS

A major result of the breakup of the Soviet Union in August 1991 was the so-called "peace dividend" that reduced the need for the Western powers to maintain such a high profile national defense structure. In order not to anticipate too much too soon from a situation that had not prevailed for five decades, the United States relaxed its state of alert around the world at a slow pace. A major restructuring of the US Air Force, implemented on June 1, 1992, resulted in the formation of Air Combat Command and Air Mobility Command. However, the headlines soon shifted from an inert Cold War to smaller, very active, "hot wars." Several conflicts, each on a scale that was minute in comparison to the deadly, nuclear-tipped threat that war with the Eastern bloc had presented, have nevertheless involved US intervention in the two decades since "Glasnost" and "Perestroika" first became familiar words. In the most recent war in Afghanistan, the US made a significant commitment and while Somalia and Bosnia remain quiet, the embers of war are glowing still in the Persian Gulf.

Despite the fact that these were limited conflicts, they have still presented a potential threat if not to world peace then local stability. The US-led coalition that fought in the Gulf reinforced the need to maintain the flexibility inherent in air, sea, and naval forces in the early years after the Cold War and air power still remains at the cutting edge of the Western world's ability to retaliate where military targets are clearly identified.

Restructuring

The closure of bases, mergers in the aerospace industry, and major restructuring were three major results of the end of the Cold War for the US Air Force. In place of the old Tactical and Strategic Air Commands and their clearly defined spheres of responsibility, an integrated Air Combat Command, which to many represents the biggest shake-up that the USAF has ever undergone, brings together the various tactical and strategic strike elements. The AMC directs the passive but vital support of transport, intelligence, and flight refueling units. Despite restructuring and

RIGHT: Modern fighter pilots wear a "bone dome" helmet with an antiglare visor. A current trend is to mount sights on the helmet, thereby reducing workload still further .

BROWN

ABOVE: US Navy deck handlers prepare an F/A-18 Hornet for launching. The lack of ordnance on the aircraft suggests one of the hundreds of training flights a carrier conducts on every cruise.

RIGHT: Larger visual displays that monitor aircraft state closely are replacing analog instruments in modern combat aircraft cockpits, that of the F/A-18 being very "state of the art."

downsizing its vast military machine in the last years of the 20th century, the US actually lost little of its combat capability, due mainly to the debut of a number of new weapons and systems. Provided that a battlefield continues to exist, the US can still demonstrate its awesome strike capability.

Although the peace dividend brought about a significant reduction in overall military aircraft numbers compared to the 1970s and 1980s, the USAF inventory of 2002/2003 includes highly sophisticated stealth aircraft such as the F-117 fighter and B-2 bomber. In stark contrast are the old stagers such the AC-130, based on a transport that first flew in 1954. The stealth types have more than made up in capability for the retirement of aircraft perceived to be obsolescent or uneconomical in terms of further technical upgrades.

An overriding factor in the post Cold War atmosphere was a "need for less," which extended to bases and entire military units as well as aircraft numbers. However, this view was certainly not shared by numerous generals and admirals. In budgetary terms, a streamline military force made sense, but the events of September 11, 2001, and the appalling destruction of the World Trade Center, New York, must have convinced many that the US can and should adopt an even higher defense posture. The subsequent pursuit of Osama bin Laden into Afghanistan adds weight to any argument for maintaining strong military forces and the future hardly heralds lasting peace in many areas of the world.

Inventory

In addition to the highly sophisticated aircraft that carry them, current 21st-century, US air-launched munitions have an improved, "all purpose" nature by combining the capability of several different classes of weapon. And to the undoubted satisfaction of the Congressional budget holders, the weapons of today are increasingly developed for use by all US services. This is not exactly a new concept but one that will clearly be expanded upon in the future. The words "joint" and "triple service" appear increasingly in the

ABOVE: Old though it is today, the 2.75-in (70-mm) rocket packed into convenient multiround pods still constitutes an impressive weapon against certain categories of ground target. Here a US Navy F/A-18 unleashes a full salvo from each wing station.

identifying acronyms of certain types of hardware, much of it associated with stealth aircraft, which unlike more traditional aircraft cannot be festooned with pods, tanks, bombs, and missiles on external racks. In the coming years, stealth capability will undoubtedly be extended to other aircraft and weapons; cruise missiles such as the AGM-129 have received the treatment and been adapted to boost its low rate of detection during a 1,800-mile target run. Research continues to extend stealth capability to the AGM-137, the shorter range Tri-Service Stand Off Attack Missile (TSAAM).

Historically the single-seat strike aircraft has been the cornerstone of tactical air power and, despite conceding some of this exclusivity to the helicopter, most recent conflicts have incorporated a high proportion of fixed-wing tactical strike aircraft, at least in the early stages. When Iraq invaded the small Gulf state of Kuwait in August 1990, the US led a coalition of 30 nations to restore Kuwait's independence. Operation "Desert Storm" opened with an intensive round of "first strike" sorties with the primary aim of destroying or at least significantly reducing the enemy's ability to mount retaliatory air attacks. With loss of radar, and missile and gun defenses in total disarray, Iraq's air force proved to be a paper tiger. The expected large-scale threat from that quarter never materialized, despite the Iraqi air force's potentially strong inventory of modern warplanes built around a core of highly capable Soviet types. Having taken the initiative, the coalition of Western allied countries never lost it and succeeding operations were outstandingly successful.

Blanket aerial surveillance via orbiting AWACs enabled the workhorse F-15 and F-16 to demonstrate that large-scale USAF counter air operations, confined within sensitive national boundaries, present few problems. The F-15 and F-16 had been deployed for many years in a continuing front-line combat role by Israel, but war in the Gulf was the first on such a scale to involve modern fast jets with American personnel. An overwhelming coalition force was ranged against Iraq, supported by extensive and effective ECM and ELINT sorties to disable defense radar. In a conflict where it was impossible to predict the degree of resistance, in the event American fighters and bombers were able to work virtually unmolested.

It would be wrong to underestimate the part played by Allied air forces, particularly the RAF, which undertook many hazardous airfield strikes at minimum altitude; a "high risk" tactic that the USAF all but abandoned after the Vietnam War. The principal reason was that strike aircraft should no longer have to go in at low levels and expose themselves to a hostile defense network if precision-guided munitions could be relied on at a stand-off position. The downside of this argument is the enormous cost of weapons used to destroy low-tech targets such as bunkers. Wars rarely develop in the way that arms manufacturers predict and along with the vagaries of actual combat, variables of weather conditions, enemy defenses, accuracy of target information, and electronics malfunction, these are factors that cannot yet ensure a "one shot, one hit" situation.

A different type of war to that in the Gulf confronted the USAF, Navy, and Marine air units in Bosnia. Deployed initially in a familiar opening phase of intensive strategic air strikes, this NATO-brokered offensive soon peaked, to be replaced by that of peacekeeping in the form of armed reconnaissance patrols to enforce a "no-fly" zone. Fast jet pilots found less and less worthwhile targets in an area that boasted few active missile and gun defenses and could only wait for the painstaking effort on the ground to work through to the opposing sides agreeing truce terms that finally held.

The air action in Bosnia and Kosovo underscored the importance of cooperation by countries friendly to the US in terms of territorial overflight agreements and use of air bases. Operations in the Balkans were particularly aided by the use of Incirlik in Turkey, where the majority of air strikes were mounted from. Bases along the Saudi Arabian coast – Doha, Al Jaber, and All al Salem – together with King

BELOW: S-3A Viking aircraft of Air Antisubmarine Squadron 38 refuels over the Sierra Nevada Mountains. It remain an integral part of any strike force undertaking secondary support roles aboard USN carriers

Khalid and Al Kharj near the capital Riyadh, also enabled US air forces to carry out strikes into Iraq. The US Central Command, which has its headquarters in Florida, has responsibility for operations in the Middle East and South Asia. Nicknamed the "Sandbox," it is controlled from its forward headquarters at Prince Sultan Air Base (also near Riyadh). When "Desert Storm" ended, overflights of Iraq remained necessary to ensure the terms of the ceasefire were adhered to and these bases continued to be very active. The subsequent antiterrorist conflict in Afghanistan, Operations "Enduring Freedom" and "Bright Star," recorded a further increase in the use of foreign bases by US air forces in that region. Thanks to international agreements a limited number of US aircraft have access to bases in Pakistan, Uzbekistan, and Tajikstan.

Afghanistan has some similarities with the Balkans conflict. It has highly difficult terrain in which to pinpoint targets, relatively few effective AA weapons, and a general lack of airborne opposition, meaning that securing a conclusion to the war has not been completely trouble free. Tactical air power has been somewhat overshadowed by the need for strategic battlefield attack by heavy bombers in deference to the well dug-in positions manned by Al Qaida forces. Historically a very difficult country to subdue (as the Red Army found to its cost), Afghanistan's terrain has offered far less hindrance to air strikes than it would to ground armies. The Taliban appear to have met their match as a result of large-scale American bombing of otherwise invulnerable hill positions and underground complexes.

Even though bunker-busting was probably not envisaged as a primary role for the B-2 Spirit, the US has demonstrated its incredible capacity not only to spend billions of dollars on the world's most advanced aircraft, but to deploy them in combat. The B-2 could be seen as a throwback to a Cold War scenario, intended for retaliatory strikes on "hard" targets such as strategic missiles sites, power stations, factories, and petrol, oil, and lubricant (POL) production facilities. However, recent US combat sorties have been mainly against targets with far less resilience, difficult natural terrain aside. In explanation, so lengthy is the gestation period of modern weapons that it is all but inevitable that projections about roles and required numbers will have changed

BELOW: Compact and fitted with a folding fin to enable it to fit into carrier hangers, the S-3A/B Viking ASW aircraft entered USN service in 1974.

by the time they enter service. Bearing that in mind, it remains to be seen whether the USAF will be allowed to order an even more costly replacement of the B-2 when the time comes, but a mission by just two B-2s is reckoned, by one air force general, to be equal to 32 strike aircraft, 16 fighters, 12 air defense suppression aircraft, and 15 tankers. This is the kind of cost saving that the creation of ACC was intended to confirm.

Real veteran aircraft, such as the B-52, remain in air force service as mother ships for cruise missiles, and to prove that some things do not fundamentally change, as carriers of iron bombs. The other heavy punch in the composite wing command structure is the elegant B-1 Lancer, able to operate quite independently of other forces. While the trio of USAF long-range bombers is fully capable of undertaking a nuclear strike, the delivery of conventional ordnance seems to be the requirement they need to fulfill for the foreseeable future.

At the other end of the scale, an A-10 Thunderbolt flying "down in the weeds" is formidable against almost anything that runs on wheels or tracks while dedicated "mud movers," such as the F-15E, can deny large areas of territory to an enemy in a very short time.

With four air services to budget for, the Pentagon has also been obliged to trim the air inventories of the Navy, Marines, and the Army. Here, too, new weapons systems have enabled a greater degree of standardization and the packing of a greater punch into an existing airframe. The Navy has actually broadened its carrier-borne fighter and strike capability by developing the A/F-18 to the point that the strike tasks previously handled by the decommissioned A-6 Intruder and A-7 Corsair II are now largely embraced by the highly capable Hornet. The EA-6B Prowler electronic warfare aircraft remains an integral part of the carrier strike force as does the S-3B Viking in the ASW role, plus helicopter and fixed wing support aircraft.

The carrier task forces and the mighty F-14 Tomcat remain the tip of the naval spear. However, a percentage reduction in the number of first line fighter and strike aircraft, previously vested in several types on a carrier deck, to just two, makes the task of combat missions easier and has some economies in terms of servicing.

BELOW: A US Marine directs a EA-6B Prowler to a spot on the ramp at Aviano Air Base, Italy, as the aircraft returns from a NATO Operation Allied Force mission.

ABOVE: A "Gray Ghost" AC-130E Hercules being held in a typical left bank to sight the guns as the twin 1.6-in (40-mm) Bofors open fire during a Vietnam combat mission.

As the only US service to operate the British Aerospace Harrier, the Marines have participated in an ongoing upgrade program for the aircraft. They have taken advantage of the development potential realized by the "big wing" APG-65 radar-equipped Harrier II Plus, which has a 30ft 4in (9.24m) span compared with 25ft 3in (7.7m) of the AV-8B. The larger wing certainly makes the aircraft more combat-capable by increasing stores provision. In late 1998, VMA-214 Black Sheep was selected as the first West Coast unit to receive this variant. Over 200 Harriers remain in the inventory of a force that exists to carry out the primary duty of supporting Marine ground forces. This it does in company with conventional strike aircraft, attack, and transport helicopters which are embarked where necessary, aboard Marine carriers. During more recent events, however, Marine Harriers have been used in combat overseas without a significant Corps ground dimension.

The US Army's helicopter fleet, once larger than many of the world's entire air arms, continues to be streamlined, but again no real lack of attack capability is apparent. Vesting much in broadening the weapons load of its flagship type the AH-64 Apache, the Army has found an able replacement for its original helicopter gunship, the AH-1 Huey Cobra.

At the opposite end of the dimensional scale is the latest development of the fixed wing gunship, the Lockheed/Rockwell AC-130U Spectre. Sired in Vietnam from earlier Hercules adaptations, the AC-130U is but one of a family of modifications of the original aircraft that began in 1965. Special missions variants currently in service with the USAF encompass the roles of tanker, special forces support, and SAR.

Conventional ground forces have been partially sidelined by the increasing adoption of suicide bombings by civilian zealots, which are hard to contain, and air forces too are being sidelined, but in a more positive manner. The development of unmanned Remotely Piloted Vehicles (RPVs) to survey battlefields and convey intelligence information without any risk to human aircrew has been significantly demonstrated in Afghanistan by the General Atomics Predator. Deploying RPVs successfully was but the first step to providing them with their own weapons. Predator carries Hellfire ASMs to attack targets on an "instant update" basis from data supplied by the craft's own computers. Such deployments show a definite swing away from the traditional tactical role of manned aircraft. The attractive "expendability factor" of the RPV has finally proven its worth after decades of testing and theoretical projections of their value in combat. It is certain that increased use will be made of such surveillance systems as the necessary technology expands.

F-117

Dramatically different to any other previous single seat fighter, the Lockheed F-117 Nighthawk or "Black Jet" was the first practical result from years of technological development – much of it clandestine in nature – that enabled the radar signature of an aircraft to be reduced almost to zero. Powered by two non-afterburning General Electric F404 engines which feature "platypus" exhausts to reduce infrared signature, the unique appearance of the F-117 is due entirely to its stealth role. Covered in various radar absorbent material (RAM) coatings and with doors and panels without straight lines to deflect radar energy in all directions, the F-117 is unmistakable. Although quite ungainly on the ground, the aircraft manages to become an angular dart with dramatic purpose once in the air.

First issued to the 37th Fighter Wing, the F-117 represented the most costly development program for a fighter to date. It was so technically advanced that it appeared to guarantee its development costs would be recouped by proving that stealth design and materials actually work. Coupled with a capability unequaled by any other aircraft in this class, the advent of the Nighthawk was all but inevitable once the technical challenges had been overcome. Entering combat earlier than many generals might have predicted, the first F-117s departed for Saudi Arabia on August 20, 1990 in response to the Iraqi invasion. Flown by crews of the 37th Fighter Wing, the Nighthawk's participation in Operation "Desert Shield/Storm" was highly successful by all accounts.

To support Operation "Allied Force," the NATO bombing campaign over the former Yugoslavia, the 49th FW deployed 25 of its F-117s to Aviano Air Base in Italy. From there the US stealth fighters attacked high priority targets in Serbia and Kosovo.

Combat over the disputed Balkans was not without loss, however, even for the very high tech F-117. Serb SAM missiles were launched in response to Allied air attacks on Belgrade and on the night of March 28/29, 1999, one apparently struck home, bringing down a Nighthawk of the 49th FW. The pilot was rescued.

On the credit side, the F-117A proved highly capable of delivering precision munitions in the face of intense AAA fire over Iraq. The aircraft carries all

BELOW: The F-117A Stealth Fighter is the first operational aircraft conceived to exploit low-observable stealth technology. It is flown by pilots of the Tactical Air Command's 37th Tactical Fighter Wing.

stores in an internal weapons bay and in deference to its stealth role, lacks a built-in gun. The last of 59 production F-117As was completed in August 1982.

ABOVE: A huge amount of money and faith has gone into the F-22 Raptor. Designed to serve for much of the 21st century, it represents one of the largest military contracts since the end of the Cold War.

F-22 and Joint Strike Fighter

The trend toward integrated weapons systems deployable by a wide range of first line aircraft has led to the concept of a single airframe able to serve in a diversity of roles for different services. The F-22 Raptor, the next generation air dominance fighter, is intended initially to replace the single seat F-15C and later the F-15E and F-117 strike fighters. Fulfillment of the latter plan by the F-22 is years away and could well be overtaken by procurement of the even more advanced X-35 Joint Strike Fighter (JSF). The intention is clear. After the mergers of the US aviation industry that were at least unlikely during the Cold War, one or two strike fighter projects that handle every conceivable combat situation can benefit from the expert input of several companies. As a result the JSF is on course to be the largest military project ever developed by the US.

Lockheed and Northrop were the original contractors for the Advanced Tactical Fighter (ATF), which became the F-22. General Dynamics and Boeing subsequently collaborated to beat the rival F-23 from Northrop McDonnell Douglas. The F-22 flew for the first time on September 29, 1990. The USAF selection of an F-22, powered by two Pratt & Whitney F119-PW-100 afterburning turbojets, followed in April 1991. Two development aircraft were flying by June 1998 and the Air Force currently plans to procure 339 aircraft, with Initial Operating Capability (IOC) testing scheduled.

Despite incorporating a significant degree of stealth technology, such as undetectable and radar

RIGHT: A US Navy version of the Joint Strike Fighter. The JSF is the military's next generation, multirole, strike aircraft designed to complement the Navy F/A-18 and USAF F-22.

absorbent material, construction of the F-22 marks a return to a more conventional design layout compared to the radical F-117. Broadly similar in configuration to the F/A-18, the aircraft's construction has serrated panel and door edges to help deflect radar energy. This is reported to give a radar signature the size of a bee, and enables the Raptor to avoid detection by the most sophisticated air defense systems. The extreme agility the aircraft achieves is built around a power to weight ratio of 1.4 to 1, compared to the 1 to 1 ratio of the F-16.

In terms of combat capability the Raptor has been designed to defeat all current (and projected) fighters in aerial combat under the "first look, first kill" philosophy. Fixed armament is retained in the form of an internal long-barreled GE M61AI Vulcan cannon with up to four AIM-9s in side weapons bays. Ventral bays accommodate four AIM-120A Amraams or six AIM-120Cs. A secondary role is that of precision ground attack with JDAM PGMs including GBU-32. The future of the F-22, as with any modern combat aircraft, depends on it passing stringent performance, avionics, and weapons integration tests. Overriding everything is the cost. Each F-22 is expected to have a price tag of at least $83 million; adding research and development and support may push the figure per aircraft to $173 million. The USAF, and particularly Congress, will press for an across the board clean bill of health as to the aircraft's capabilities. In short the Raptor's manufacturers have to make it one of the most capable aircraft of all time.

One problem the Air Force faces in its ongoing battles for a military budget elastic enough to absorb inflation projections for aircraft and systems, which are as yet unproven, is the fact that no one aircraft can quite meet all requirements. Air Force chiefs made a case for a future inventory with the emphasis on F-22s and the production of the X-35, wanting to obtain 1,763 of the latter. The US Navy requirement was quoted as 480, the US Marines 609, and a further 150 to equip the British Royal Air Force and Royal Navy.

The JSF, similar in configuration to the F-22, began life as an F-16, F/A-18, and AV-8 replacement. Powered by a single P&W SE611 turbofan, an F-119 derivative, the X-35 is both land and carrier based and adaptable to Short Take-off Vertical Landing (STOVL) via an Allison engine driven lift fan

LEFT: An artist's impression of the US Navy's version of the Joint Strike Fighter. The development program is a joint US–UK effort to affordably replace aging strike assets.

mounted behind the cockpit. This is a system that can be adapted to later more advanced configuration. An internal gun is planned for the USAF version, with AIM-9X, AIM-120, and JDAMs arming the US versions across the board.

Confirmation for the X-35 to enter production came in December 2001, beating the Lockheed Martin design for the unconventional Boeing X-32 that still required further development. One factor that is believed to have helped the case for the X-35 is that the design was virtually fixed and did not require an unspecified sum for further refinement. A figure of 6,000 X-35s was estimated for the world market as the project entered its System Development and Demonstration (SDD) phase of 126 months.

LEFT: Modern aircraft gun technology remains with the principle of multiple revolving barrels to aid cooling. The M61A1 79-in (20-mm) cannon in the F-16 has its ammunition coiled in a drum to save space.

F-15

Big, powerful, hugely expensive, and not without early teething troubles, the mighty Eagle grew to be a potent symbol of the modern USAF. As with most current, highly sophisticated combat aircraft it was closely scrutinized by Congress in its time and was inevitably regarded as too costly. But with "the threat" looming large the Eagle was pushed through. One of its attributes as far as the Air Force was concerned was that the F-15 restored the time-honored single seat fighter concept that had, at least for that service, been somewhat compromised by the two-seat Phantom. Failing to plan its F-4 crew integration as well as the Navy did, the USAF found itself with some serious challenges to morale, particularly in Vietnam. After the war, technical progress in control and monitoring systems enabled the F-15's pilot's workload to be reduced so that it could be flown comfortably by one occupant. Highly successful peacetime integration into tactical air defense and strike wings around the world made the Eagle an Air Force cornerstone, its lengthy service record punctuated by several bouts of combat.

All the computer-simulated, combat scenarios in the world pale into insignificance at the point where an real enemy aircraft is indicated on the head up display. Flown by pilots, who can be very unpredictable in an unreal, undeclared "war skirmish" situation, the F-15's challengers have invariably been Russian MiGs and Sukhois. These challengers have rarely gained the upper hand, but in such situations Eagle drivers have had to engage in one-on-one maneuvering after ensuring that a "Mk. I eyeball" rather than a beyond line of sight missile computer has made positive identification.

All the missile kills in the Gulf War were made by F-15Cs which were ably supported by the crews of the E-3 AWACS who passed range, position, and number coordinates of Iraqi interceptors to the fighter pilots. Of the F-15 missiles expended, 24 kills were made by the Sparrow and 12 by the Sidewinder, with one kill unconfirmed

The Eagle gained a second crew member that of the F-15E, which fortuitously met an early 1980s

requirement for a new multirole fighter under the Advanced Tactical Fighter (ATF) program to supplement the F-111 strike aircraft. The F-15E was selected in February 1984, and its first flight was in December 1986. Disparagingly known as the "mud mover" Eagle to some, the F-15E is highly capable in a ground attack role. Its systems include an APG-70 radar with ground mapping, including seven multifunction CRTs and laser target acquisition, which combine to accurately position the aircraft and achieve the most effective use of its substantial ordnance load of up to 24,500lb (11,113kg).

ABOVE: An AIM-7 Sparrow radar-guided missile, seconds after launching from a 318th FIS F-15A Eagle. Despite a checkered combat career this missile remains an integral part of the US ordnance inventory.

BELOW: Pave Mover's data link and radar components ride in a special pallet-pod, mounted in the bomb bay of an F-111E during evaluation tests at White Sands Missile Range, New Mexico.

ABOVE LEFT: An F-15 Eagle is prepared for launching from Tyndall Air Force Base, Florida.

LEFT: Bombs are loaded onto an F-15 at Aviano Air Base, Italy.

ABOVE: A USAF F-15E takes off from Incirlik Air Base, Turkey.

RIGHT: Preflight checks are performed on precision guided munitions loaded on an F-15E.

F-16

"Electric Jet," "Viper," or even the official Fighting Falcon are names used to describe this outstandingly capable single-seater from General Dynamics. The F-16, in common with most other contemporary combat aircraft, has proven to be highly adaptable to new and improved systems without compromising performance, despite the inevitable weight increase that such changes bring. Evaluation and service has continued since the Viper's first production in 1975 and it is still included in plans for the foreseeable future. The F-16 remains one of the most economical and capable fighters operated by the USAF and the general goal of integrating the type's avionics suite across the different production blocks is currently reflected in the Air Force's Common Configuration Implementation Program (CCIP). Around 700 F-16 Block 40/42s and 50/52s are to be modified, and the latter series of aircraft will also receive PGM targeting pods.

Such upgrades to extend airframe life may mean that the F-16 and other types will be prematurely replaced by the new F-22s of Air Combat Command. That remains to be seen but the USAF maintains numerous slots for upgraded combat aircraft in its Reserve Force and the Air Guard. These are formations that have previously extended the useful life of "nearly new" types in America's highly capable second line forces.

Under Air Combat Command, F-16s have tended to undertake a more diverse role than they had as part of TAC. Nowadays a missile-laden Viper on an

BELOW: Small but highly capable, the F-16 has been a key USAF strike fighter since the mid 1970s. Upgrades will ensure it a place in Air Combat Command inventory for the foreseeable future.

LEFT: AN F-16CJ Fighting Falcon at Incirlik Air Base, Turkey, after an Operation "Northern Watch" mission enforcing the northern no-fly zone over Iraq.

BELOW: First Penguin missile launch from an F-16 conducted over the Pacific Missile Test Range in 1986. The missile is beginning to separate from the wing pylon.

BOTTOM: Moments after the launch of the Penguin, the missile is approximately 70ft below the aircraft.

antiradar/SAM suppression mission will usually carry its own ECM and targeting equipment in underwing pods rather than rely on a Wild Weasel (historically an F-4) to set up the target for its AGM-88 or similar antiradiation missiles. Equipment pods have of course long been an integral part of such single-seaters and back up is invariably available if necessary. Here again, economy is the keynote but the revised Air Force policy provides fighter pilots with a greater appreciation of the increasing importance of tactical targets and the flight profiles and weapons required to neutralize them.

B-1 Lancer

A straight spelling-out of the B-1's designation produces the word "Bone," the nickname both air and ground crews have universally adopted to describe the Lancer. With a design that goes back to 1971, the elegant B-1A and its distinctive variable geometry wing faced an uncertain future when the Carter administration suspended production in 1977. Regenerated by Ronald Reagan in 1981, the elegant B-1B appeared to be a highly capable replacement for the USAF's aging B-52. It was, but only in part. Advanced and expensive, the B-1 was in its second manifestation, confirmed for a multi-purpose, high or low level attack role. Budget restrictions keep only 75 of the 95 B-1s in service (100 were ordered) on call at any one time. However, having made its

combat debut over Iraq during Operation "Desert Fox" in 1998, the Bone also went onto action over Kosovo the following year. Operation "Allied Force" showed that, for all their saber-rattling, Serb forces were incapable of adequately defending targets such as the Novi Sad oil refinery. This was heavily bombed by two B-1s that were operating out of RAF Fairford, England on May 1, 1999.

The sophisticated B-1 has proven a little more difficult to integrate into ACC than some other types principally because it is very expensive to operate. Fortunately it is also quite capable of carrying out missions alone, and for that reason Bone crews tend to undertake specific tasks separate to those performed by the rest of their parent Wings and to operate singly at low, medium, or high altitudes depending on the mission.

Whatever the mission of the B-1 the Air Force (in common with other contemporary types) has largely dispensed with the hauling of individual bombs out to the aircraft. Now that its role as a nuclear deterrent role has been shelved, the B-1 utilizes a Conventional Munitions Module (CMM) which is pre-loaded with up to 26 x 500lb (227kg) Mk. 82 general purpose bombs. If necessary the Bone can take three CMMs and further stores, including AGM-86B cruise missiles, on external racks for a maximum load. This may sound impressive but the reality is that scattering sticks or strings of bombs over a target area is a tactic from the days of nuclear strikes, when the allowable margin of error was understandably quite large. That mission profile ran counter to ACC philosophy and for a time Bone crews under-

LEFT: Elegant and able, the B-1 is the mighty "Bone" to its fiercely loyal crews. Designed as a B-52 replacement it has created its own role as an integrated weapons in the current USAF.

RIGHT: An airman rolls a Mk. 82 bomb to the end of the bomb trailer as the munitions crew loads a B-52H Stratofortress.

BELOW RIGHT: A USAF B1-B Lancer bomber from the 28th Bomb Squadron is loaded with Mk. 82 bombs.

took a degree of retraining to reemphasize precision bombing, which the aircraft achieves by utilizing the Global Positioning System (GPS) and Inertial Navigation System (INS) guided versions of the Mk. 80 gravity bomb. By fitting this "dumb bomb" with a guidance system in the tail section, a target accuracy of within 45ft (13.7m) can be achieved. Other modular weapons and a range of JDAMs make the B-1 a very versatile long range bomber, and a single machine is capable of delivering an impressive degree of destruction.

B-2

At the cutting edge of US strategic striking power is the dramatic B-2 Spirit, which has a zigzag "all-wing" stealth design to endow it with virtual immunity from defensive guns and missiles.

With the availability of tankers on a 24-hour basis, the USAF no longer has any problems in deploying aircraft that *per se* have limited range. Types such as the B-2 have to be able to fly sorties to anywhere in the world, as recent conflicts have shown. During Afghan operations in October 2001, a single B-2 of the 509th Bomb Wing took off from Whitemam Air Force Base in western Missouri. Some 44 hours later the aircraft had flown 7,000 miles (11,265 km) and delivered 16 JDAMs on several targets including airstrips, inside Afghanistan. The entire B-2 operation is virtually automatic, and the crew only fly the Spirit off the runway, carry out the designated mission, and land it. The rest of the flight is conducted on autopilot, a flight profile that was deliberately planned according to the crews, to be "monotonous and boringly easy." To offset this on extreme duration

LEFT: Covered in mats to prevent the work force causing any degradation of their sensitive stealth surfaces, B-2 Spirits are seen in the final phase of assembly at Northrop.

BELOW LEFT: A B-2 Spirit has its flying surfaces tested while taxiing out for take-off. To retain stealth integrity external stores cannot be used on this type of aircraft.

missions B-2 crews operate in shifts. As the Air Force dislikes leaving the aircraft on overseas bases because of security considerations and the fact that any maintenance they might require is highly specialized, fresh crews are positioned for the return leg to the States. On the above Afghan sortie the Spirit flew to Diego Garcia in the Indian Ocean, where a relief crew of two took over to fly it back to Missouri.

With 21 Spirits budgeted for (against the original USAF requirement for 133) production was completed in 1997. Even this modest build required a total of US$45 billion, including development costs.

B-52

A weapon popularly associated with serious intent by the US to bring about a result in a difficult tactical situation, the aged B-52 has proven to be a very effective means of persuasion. The Stratofortress has been continually upgraded and is all but decisive in its ability to saturate targets that have proved impervious to small scale ordnance delivered by more conventional means. The current B-52 fleet of 90 plus "short tail" H models represents a milestone of development in that eight 17,000lb (7,711kg), Pratt & Whitney TF-33 turbofans are able to boost the aircraft's range by a third compared to that possible with turbojets.

TOP: A USAF B-2A Spirit bomber approaches the refueling boom of a KC-135R Stratotanker as the two aircraft rendezvous over Alaska for an in-flight refueling procedure.

LEFT: A symbol of American airpower for more than four decades, the B-52's life extension program will see it through several more before final retirement. This B-52G has inboard racks for various loads including cruise missiles.

ABOVE: A pilot of a USAF B-52H Stratofortress scans the horizon for aircraft as he flies in formation with another B-52 on a combat penetration mission toward a target in Kosovo.

LEFT: A B-52H Stratofortress receives fuel through the refueling boom of a KC-10 Extender aerial tanker during in-flight refueling over the Indian Ocean.

RIGHT: Members of the 96th Bomber Maintenance Squadron perform post-mission maintenance on a USAF B-52 Stratofortress bomber at Andersen Air Force Base, Guam.

RIGHT: A USAF airman positions the bomb load truck as members of a weapons load crew prepare to attach a AGM-65 Maverick missile to the wing of an A-10 Thunderbolt II.

FAR RIGHT: The snout of the A-10 Thunderbolt II contains the seven barrel '"business end" of the giant Avenger 1.2-in (30-mm) cannon that is the aircraft's sole fixed armament.

Further engine upgrades are anticipated, possibly using Rolls-Royce RB-211-535s with 43,200lb (19,596kg) thrust, to keep the B-52 in inventory until 2034. If that does indeed prove to be the case, the B-52 will by then have been in service a staggering 79 years (since 1955).

The B-52's maximum load of up to 51 x 750lb (340kg) iron bombs has been enhanced by weapons that are singularly devastating against certain types of structures and terrain. One of these is the AGM-142 Popeye stand-off fire and forget missile, a rare US foreign "buy in," from Rafael of Israel in this case.

The Stratofortress has been successfully integrated into the ACC force structure, as recent combat operations have shown, and the B-52, that shares saturation bombing missions with the B-2, remains an integral part of the USAF's current strategy.

A-10

Historically the dedicated antiarmor aircraft has been a difficult requirement to meet; contenders often lacked the ability to lift enough ordnance or to demonstrate a high enough degree of combat survival. The A-10 Thunderbolt II (otherwise known as Warthog) met the requirement on all these counts and has proved a useful investment for the USAF. Whereas almost any type can be adapted for a specific ground attack role, anticipated high attrition in combat quickly cancels out all but the toughest and most agile of aircraft.

Adopting a low-wing configuration that would provide both an ample number of stores (on 11 hardpoints) while serving to shield the engines mounted on the rear fuselage from ground fire, Fairchild's design also incorporated the largest fixed gun ever fitted to this class of aircraft. This is the 1.2-in (30mm) GAU-8, seven-barrel cannon, which manufacturers General Electric once posed with a VW Beetle to show it was longer than even a family car.

A titanium armor "bathtub" cockpit section offers ample protection to the pilot. The aircraft is designed to lift 16,000lb (7,258kg) of ordnance and demonstrate a loitering time of up to 1 hour 42 minutes. When it entered a combat situation during the Gulf War, the A-10 excelled under harsh conditions, similar to those repeated in Afghanistan.

The 707th example completed the production of the A-10 and although less than half that number currently remain in USAF service, the Warthog has more than proved its usefulness. Its basic attack role has been expanded into that of Forward Air Control, OA-10s carrying smoke marker rockets, and AIM-9 AAMs for self defense.

ABOVE: The humped cockpit identifies this Thunderbolt II as a single conversion intended to meet a night/ all weather attack role in which the second cockpit was filled with electronic equipment.

BELOW: High-vis 'stars and bars' markings confirm this A-10 photo as an early 1970s view of an AIM-4 Falcon missile test. For its attack role the "Warthog" tested all weapons in USAF inventory.

AC-130

The AC-130 gunship, another USAF aircraft of the "old guard" remaining from the vast air inventory of the Vietnam War period, is presently operated by the 16th Special Operations Squadron from the original SOS base, Hurlburt Field in Florida. The gunship unit currently flying the AC-130U Specter/Spooky nicknames this venerable old Hercules variant the "U-boat." Chock full of electronics, guns and ammunition, the AC-130 has been deployed on most of the occasions that the US military has seen action since the Southeast Asian conflict. Able to deluge an area the size of a football pitch with thousands of rounds of automatic weapons fire, the Specter has to be flown "low and slow" and the pilot holds it in a bank over the target area. This inevitably exposes the aircraft to ground defenses and since eight were lost in Southeast Asia, combat over Kuwait and Somalia (in 1994) has claimed a further two.

ABOVE: Large enough to pack in a comprehensive electronics suite as well as a battery of machineguns and cannon, the AC-130 gunship made its combat debut in Vietnam.

LEFT: Ground view of an AC-130E in all black paintwork which emphasized its clandestine ECM/gunship role that remains part of current Air Force inventory.

Support Force

The all important USAF support forces encompassing trainers, transports, and tankers continue to be upgraded. Stretched C-130J-30s have been incorporated at the 143d Airlift Wing of the Rhode Island Air National Guard at Quonset State Airport. Each of the new Hercules features the computer-controlled Enhanced Cargo Handling System, which allows airdrops to be carried out with greater precision than has hitherto been possible with the C-130J. In addition, the new variant meets Army/Air Force requirements for the safe deployment of up to 128 paratroops from both sides of the aircraft.

Tankers

As the ranges over which tactical strike aircraft operate have tended to be extended and the USAF's fleet of venerable KC-135s of Air Mobility Command are still being upgraded, tankers have taken on a steadily increasing importance in recent years. The established reengining program continues and the Flight Refueling Mk. 32B underwing pod is currently being fitted to an initial 35 examples. This Multipoint Refueling System (MPRS) gives the Air Force's first jet tanker the capability to simultaneously transfer fuel to Navy aircraft using the probe and drogue system and USAF machines operating the fixed flying boom. Although the Stratotanker was previously able to fulfill such duel refueling, it was only possible by deploying more than one aircraft. A drogue attached to the boom enabled Navy aircraft to fill up, but a single tanker could not switch to the Air Force system while in flight.

As well as operating the KC-135 and KC-10 Extender, the Air Force is hoping to finalize a ten year, $20bn lease arrangement with the manufacturer covering 100 Boeing 767s. The Boeing 767s will supplement the KC-135s, some 150 of which equip the 22nd, 92nd, and 319th Air Refueling Wings.

The US Navy

In the early stages of impending military action abroad, power projection for the United States is usually vested in elements of her fleet aircraft carriers. The mere presence of one or more of these mighty warships, unrivaled in size and strike capability, is enough to demonstrate that the nation means business. As shown in the Gulf War, once the shooting starts these vessels pack a devastating punch, as befits the world's largest navy. Investing in nine nuclear-powered carriers (with a tenth due to commission) the Pacific Fleet currently has four and the Atlantic Fleet five. Of these the USS *Enterprise* is the oldest ship to enter service and USS *Ronald Reagan* (CVN-76) the most recent. USS *Nimitz*, *Eisenhower*,

RIGHT: A US Navy A-6E from Attack Squadron 34 lines up its fuel probe with the buddy-store basket deployed by a VA-34 Intruder in preparation for in-flight refueling.

LEFT: A US Navy F-14A Tomcat releases a GBU-24B/B hard target, penetrator laser-guided bomb, while in a in a 45-degree dive.

BELOW: A Sikorsky SH-3D Sea King creating a typical "ripple" effect on the sea while "dipping" its submarine detection sonar.

ABOVE: An F/A-18E Super Hornet is loaded with two 2,000lb bombs, two AGM-88 High-Speed Antiradiation (HARM) missiles, and two AIM-9 Sidewinder missiles.

RIGHT: The highly versatile SH-60 Seahawk offers shipboard ASW capability to shield task forces from incursions by hostile submarines and carries a range of torpedoes and anti-ship missiles.

BELOW, RIGHT: Navy Seahawks perform multiple roles including ASW, rescue and commando insertion. Further upgrades in armament are currently planned.

Vinson, *Roosevelt*, *Lincoln*, *Washington*, *Stennis*, and *Harry S Truman* were progressively added throughout the intervening decades.

Each nuclear carrier now carries a complement of some 75 highly capable A/F-18 Hornets and F-14 Tomcats. These are routinely operated from Atlantic or Pacific Fleet stations on an ongoing peacetime training program and launches are carried out around the clock for crews to complete the requisite number of flight hours to maintain efficiency. With their ability to remain on station for months on end due to their highly efficient nuclear reactors, these ships have proven able to impose and maintain an essential blockade of hostile waters without direct assistance from the other US services. Backing the nuclear fleet are several conventional carriers including the USS *Constellation*, USS *John F Kennedy* (the last conventional carrier built for the navy) and USS *Kitty Hawk*.

Four battle groups built around the USS *Enterprise*, *Vinson*, *Roosevelt*, and *Kitty Hawk* (converted to a helicopter-equipped depot ship for special forces support with no jet strike capability) were most recently deployed to the Persian Gulf to operate against terrorist forces in Afghanistan.

ABOVE: Engine exhaust shielding gear enables the Sea Hawk to safely patrol "dangerous" waters during antisubmarine patrol exercises.

BELOW: Avenger typically carries four ready-to-fire Stinger missiles on each of its two arms. A forward-looking infrared unit is carried below one pod and a pair of M240 guns beneath the other. Here a Hydra-70 pod containing 19 rockets in mounted on the port arm.

F-14 Tomcat

Tasked with a Combat Air Patrol (CAP) role during the Gulf War, ten squadrons of F-14s totally succeeded in preventing any attack on the US Navy task forces. As such flights took place close to the carriers action was rare, and only a single enemy aircraft fell to Tomcat crews during the Gulf War. However, they were continually airborne and ready, watching every strike package take off.

The F-14 began such duty at the end of the Vietnam War when the VF-1 and VF-2 deployed from the USS *Enterprise*, which patrolled the South China Sea as the 1975 the evacuation known as Operation "Frequent Wind" got underway. No hostile aircraft were encountered but the cruise, which was primarily to evaluate the new fleet fighter under operational conditions, was an outstanding success. During the Vietnam withdrawal enemy ground fire had been aimed at the F-14s but no damage was inflicted.

Six years were to pass before the F-14 came close to combat action again. On August 19, 1981 the Fast Eagle flight of two Tomcats from VF-41 aboard the USS *Nimitz* engaged and shot down two hostile Libyan Su-22s. Monitoring an American naval exercise in the Gulf of Sidra, the Libyan aircraft ran in on the patrolling F-14s and one suddenly launched an Atoll AAM.

Cleared to engage, the F-14s made no mistake. Both Su-22s were dispatched by AIM-9L Sidewinder shots. Tomcats were involved in further action against the Libyan Air Force on January 4, 1989 when F-14s from *John F Kennedy* encountered two MiG-23s. Again the outcome was the same: Americans 2, Libyans 0.

Currently the status of the F-14 in the Navy reflects a broader mission profile since the retirement of the A-6 Intruder. Older F-14As remain in service along with the F-14B and F-14D, which have enhanced air-to-ground capability with digital avionics and radar processing linked to the AWG-9 radar; both the latter variants are also equipped to use the Lantirn designator pod.

The Achilles heel to what is widely regarded as the finest fleet defense fighter extant has been engines.

RIGHT: A sequence of camera frames of an F-14 launching an AIM-54 Phoenix during early compatibility trials. The six missiles carried by the Tomcat are able to deal with multiple threats almost simultaneously.

ABOVE: First of a second generation of nuclear-powered super carriers, the *Nimitz* remains a cornerstone of the US Atlantic Fleet.

RIGHT: A Tomcat comes home to roost. Even the largest carrier looks like a postage stamp until the pilot is committed to the landing and exceptional flying skill is a standard US Navy fighter pilot requirement.

The TF30 turbofan has a history of trouble, including catastrophic blade failures and was considered too underpowered to move the Tomcat's more than 30 tons weight as advertised.

Despite these drawbacks Congress refused to adequately fund the F-14B with improved P&W F401 turbofans, the first example of which made its maiden flight in 1973. The F-14B was subsequently canceled, then effectively reinstated as the F-14A (Plus) in 1984. This variant was an F-14A powered by GE 110-GE-400. It first flew in 1986, and was redesignated as the F-14B. Thirty-eight new build and 32 A model conversions were delivered. The F-14D also suffered from economies as only 37 new build and 18 rebuilds were funded.

BELOW: An artist's impression of an F-14 Tomcat firing an AIM-54 Phoenix missile with a booster attachment.

F/A-18 Hornet

As part of one of the most important aircraft programs for the modern US Navy, the first Hornet development aircraft made its maiden flight on November 18, 1978. Since then it has been built in six single- and two-seater versions and proved to be one of the most versatile aircraft ever to operate from a carrier deck. An outgrowth of the seemingly stillborn Northrop YF-17, the Hornet effectively combined the roles of fighter and ground attack, hence the distinctive designation.

Progressive upgrades have resulted in the F/A-18C with improved avionics, including a new central computer, which allowed compatibility with the AIM-120 and AGM-65. The radar fit was from 1994, the APG-73, uprated GE F404-GE-402 engines were fitted two years previously. Current Hornets are able to carry a full range of weapons – up to 15,000lb (6,804kg) – to augment their single

ABOVE: A key feature of the multi-role F/A-18E/F is its payload carrying flexibility. Here the Hornet carries one of many possible strike-fighter loads on its 11 weapon stations. From wingtips inboard are the AIM-9 Sidewinder, the AIM-120 AMRAAM, the AGM-88 HARM, and two 1,000lb (454kg) Mk. 83 bombs.

LEFT: In this sequence of photographs, an AGM-65D imaging infrared Maverick missile smashes a truck target on a test range at Eglin Air Force Base, Florida. The missile, which did not have a warhead, hit the truck parked head-on to the attacking A-10 aircraft.

M61A1 Vulcan cannon. It was F/A-18Cs that scored the Navy's two kills for the type in Operation "Desert Storm," both victories going to aircraft of VA-81 Sunliners.

The first flight of the F/A-18E Super Hornet was in November 1995, which is larger overall than the earlier models it was designed to replace in US Navy service. The original requirement for about 1,000 Super Hornets was however scaled back to 548, the last of which is scheduled to be delivered by 2010. In due course some will undoubtedly pass into Marine hands, as the Corps has been a longtime user of frontline Navy aircraft including the F/A-18.

AV-8 Harrier

The unique vertical take-off (VTO) qualities of the BAe Harrier found a ready acceptance in the Marine Corps, which saw it as an ideal type to offer fire support in amphibious landings. Delivery of 110 license-built AV-8As and two-seat TAV-8As took place in the 1970s. The AV-8A, later upgraded to AV-8C standard, was retired in 1987 because it was seen to have a rather limited capability due to its modest ordnance carrying capacity. Interest was renewed in what had in the meantime become a US rather than British-driven program, and the McDonnell Douglas/ Boeing AV-TAV-8B with an extended wing was delivered to the USMC from 1984. Five years on Marine units began to receive the AV-8B Night Attack version developed specifically for the Corps, equipped with a nose-mounted GEC Marconi forward-looking infrared (FLIR), a head-down display, and color moving map.

A detachment of six Harriers from the VMA-522 Tigers participated in the fighting in Kosovo. The aircraft flew 36 close support and reconnaissance missions and deployed Rockeye LGB and Mk. 82 munitions.

RIGHT: A steeply climbing AV-8B demonstrating the extra ordnance load possible with the extended wing. Triple clusters of Mk. 82 Snakeye bombs can be seen on the midwing pylons.

BELOW: A Night Attack AV-8B Harrier II carries laser-guided Maverick missiles, Mk. 82 500lb (227kg) bombs, and a 1-in (25mm) cannon during a test flight at 29 Palms Marine Base, California.

ABOVE: Seconds after a pair of Snakeye bombs leave the carrier aircraft, retarding fins spring open to slow them down and thus allow the fuzes time to arm and the aircraft to escape the ensuing blast.

BELOW: A Marine Corps AV-8B releases two Mk. 82 Snakeye bombs above the Nevada desert during an exercise at the Naval Air Station at Fallon. The AV-8B is equipped with an angle rate bombing system.

US Army

The deployment to Afghanistan to remove the Taliban from power in 2001–2002 put the major US Army bases, such as Fort Bragg and Fort Campbell, on a Threat Con Delta footing, the highest state of security. The latter base is home to the famed 101st Airborne Division, currently the world's only heliborne air assault division.

In a typical Afghanistan operation USAF A-10s and AC-130s provided close air support for helicopters undertaking troop insertion and rescue missions, such as the UH/EH-60A Blackhawk and MH-47 Chinook. Although the MH-47 Chinook may be armed, its sizeable configuration and relatively slow speed inevitably makes it a prime target for hostile ground forces. In Afghanistan, Al Qaida guerrillas

LEFT: Developed from the original AH-1 HueyCobra, the AH-1N has twin engines and carries a full ordnance load on stub wings.

BELOW: Angular cockpit panels hallmark the Army's AH-1S, one of which is seen here low over the trees during an antitank training sortie.

ABOVE: Despite large fuselage fairings for its twin engines, the AH-1W retains similar nose contours to the original AH-1G. The cannon is an extended barrel M-197, 0.79in (20mm) caliber.

RIGHT: A helicopter crewman getting down to the paperwork. Behind him can be seen a chain gun mounted on an AH-64.

FAR RIGHT, TOP: Awesomely ugly, the AH-64 Apache is an effective battlefield attack helicopter, able to deploy cannon fire and a range of missiles to deal with a variety of targets.

FAR RIGHT, BOTTOM: Heart of the Apache is its chain gun sight which is able to "see" the target via a gimbal-mounted rotating sight linked to the pilot's helmet-mounted sight.

occasionally inflicted damage on Chinooks with the rocket-propelled grenade (RPG), a weapon very widely deployed in the region. For more local air support with greater loiter time over a contested area, the Army can call upon its own gunships in the form of the AH-64 Apache. The amount of destruction that helicopters can achieve is necessarily limited and in the event of a protracted action on the ground with a high risk to friendly forces, USAF, Navy, and Marine fast jets could be called in to neutralize enemy positions. Operating in relays and using flight refueling where necessary, this type of air operation can be maintained for the duration of a threat, as has been proven.

The Army has begun a far-reaching Apache upgrade program under which 530 AH-64As will be converted to AH-64Ds, with improved digital avionics in enlarged cheek fairings. All but 30 will also feature the Longbow mast-mounted millimeter wave radar to guide the radio seeker built into the AGM-114 Hellfire antitank missile. Up to16 Hellfires can be accommodated by the Apache's four stub wing hardpoints which can alternatively carry rocket pods, Stinger or Sidewinders AAMs, or Sidearm ARMs.

Army AH-64D Apache Longbows were deployed to Korea in late 2001, the first such international task

ABOVE: The nose sight on an AH-1 together with podded 2.75-in (70mm) rocket rounds on each fuselage stub wing.

RIGHT: Apache lair is probably Fort Bragg, the US Army's main helicopter training base in North Carolina.

BELOW: An AH-64A Apache attack helicopter is shown armed with Hellfire antitank missiles, rocket pod, and chain gun forward of the undercarriage.

ABOVE: Agile and lethal, the AH-64 is the US Army's main attack helicopter with nearly 500 currently in service.

LEFT: The Apache's "stand off" weapons load includes 2.75-in (70mm) rockets carried in up to four pods and the Hellfire antitank missiles attached to stub wing launchers.

BELOW: A single AGM-114 Hellfire air-to-ground missile round. A practical answer to the perpetual challenge of destroying tanks with helicopters, the Hellfire's semi-active laser homer comes into play during the final phase of flight.

for the type. Initially the Longbows replaced one of three AH-64A units stationed in the country. The Apache's front line success has meant that all examples of the original helicopter gunship, the Bell AH-1, now serve with the Army Reserve and Air National Guard units.

Medium lift transport duties are being mainly handled by versions of the UH-60 Blackhawk, over 1,000 of which are in Army service. As with other US transport helicopters the Blackhawk can be armed and, as the AH-60, it can operate Miniguns or machineguns from pintle mounts in the forward cabin. It is also capable of firing Hellfire missiles or rockets from external hardpoints.

Funding restraints prevented the Army from going through with a planned engine upgrade for its 360-strong fleet of UH-1H/V Iroquois (Huey) utility helicopters, a situation that could change. However, with 838 more transport Hueys in Reserve and ANG service, the bill to upgrade them all would be substantial. It is unlikely that such a program would be carried out, as a more modern type to equip the reserve forces in the future would be preferable.

At least 300 existing airframes of the Army's medium lift Chinooks are being upgraded, however. The first CH-47F upgraded to Improved Cargo Helicopter (ICH) standard was delivered by Boeing in 2002. The Chinook remains first and foremost a transport helicopter, which can be armed if the operational scenario warrants it. Two 0.5-in (1.27mm) M2 machineguns or miniguns can be mounted in the cabin area and there is also provision available for Stinger AAMs to be carried on stub wing hardpoints if necessary.

ABOVE: AN F/A-18C Hornet launches from the waist catapult during flight operations on board the aircraft carrier USS *Nimitz* in the Persian Gulf. It is armed with a AIM-9 Sidewinder, RIM-7M Sea Sparrow, Rockeye cluster bombs, and the AGM-88 HARM.

BELOW: A B-52G bomber with its complement of 12 pylon-mounted AGM-86B Air Launched Cruise Missiles stands ready on the flight line.

Air weapons used by all services

Cruise missiles

Arguably representing the ultimate in conventional weapons is the Air Launched Cruise Missile (ALCM) which can presently be deployed only from the USAF's trio of long range bombers. This is due primarily to weight and prohibitive size, despite the fact that cruise missiles are fitted with folding wings and tailfins. The champion USAF cruise missile platform is currently the B-52, which can accommodate up to six on wing racks in addition to the internal bomb bay load—one triple rack of AGM-129A missiles weighs as much as an F-16.

The AGM-129A has now succeeded the AGM-86 cruise missile—35 of which, fitted with conventional warheads, were launched against Iraqi targets during Operation "Desert Storm." B-52Gs based at Barksdale, Lousiana, carried out the attacks, which involved round trip flight times exceeding 34 hours.

Air-to-air missiles

Although a plethora of air-to-air missiles are available for use by the world's air forces, many are variations or copies of the original, infrared, heat-seeking AIM-9 Sidewinder. The acronym stood for Aerial Intercept Missile and it was developed under a painstaking and often heartbreakingly difficult test program by technicians at the Navy test center at China Lake, California. Under the guiding hand of the irrepressible Dr William McLaren the Sidewinder IR seeker eventually "came good." The resulting series of progressively improvements gave US aircraft one of the most consistently reliable weapons of all time. The Winder program has had its disappointments, but overall its combat kill ratio has been high enough to ensure funding since February 17, 1954, the date of the first live destruction of a QB-17 drone target.

In its early AIM-9B form, the Sidewinder could only home onto the infrared radiation given off by hot metal, preferably from close range and directly behind the target aircraft. One of the greatest challenges was to provide the AIM-9 with the ability to maneuver and shoot down an aerial target even if the parent fighter launched the missile from directly ahead. AIM-9L and M versions were the first of the "all aspects" Sidewinders. The AIM-9X, contracted

ABOVE: Although it has now been phased out the F-4E Phantom was a world class fighter during the Vietnam war armed as here with a 0.79-in (20-mm) gun, AIM-7, and AIM-9 missiles.

BELOW: A ground crew loads an AIM-9 Sidewinder missile onto a F-15 Eagle at Tyndall Air Force Base, Florida.

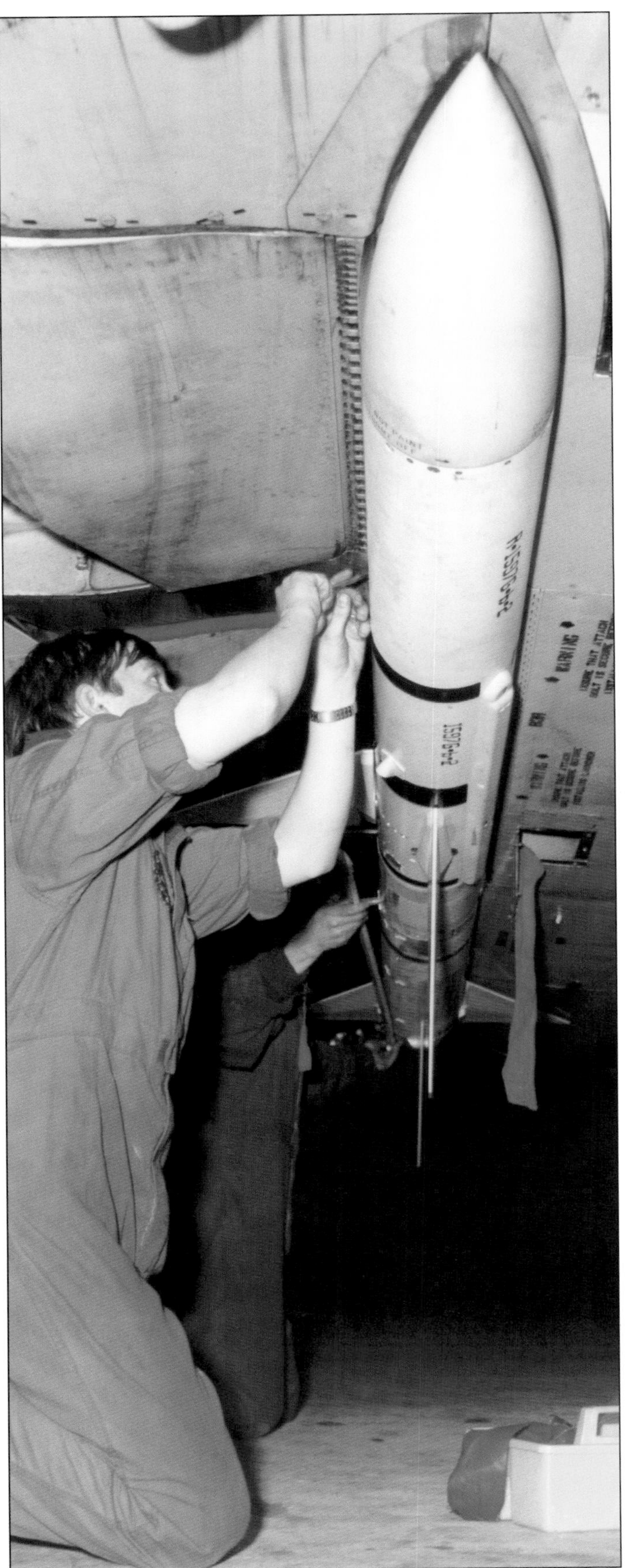

to Hughes/Raytheon, is a missile designed for short range dogfighting (which the US had neglected). It features a constant view IR array with detectors sensitive enough to track a target through all flight aspects; for the first time a Sidewinder is able to maneuver with a very fast target pulling up to 60*G* in the process. Using thrust-vector control, these next generation AAMs are also different in that they are guided by helmet-mounted sights.

The AIM-7 Sparrow went one step further than the Sidewinder in that it incorporated a tiny radar transmitter with which to home onto the returns given off by an airframe. In theory such a missile should have been far more accurate than a less sophisticated heat-seeker but this did not prove to be the case. In Vietnam, the conflict that saw the first large-scale use of AAMs as primary air weapons, pilots found that the kill ratio of Sparrow fell significantly below that of the heat-seeker. The drawback with Sparrow was its rather primitive technology and the fact that it invariably required the parent aircraft to acquire the target on radar to ensure a good missile lock-on. The attendant risk to the fighter in a combat zone was prohibitive and despite improvements, the kill ratio of the AIM-7F/M in Operation "Desert Storm" remained very low.

The AIM-120A is a replacement for the failed AIM-7 Sparrow III, known to pilots as the "Slammer," its suffix standing for Advanced Medium Range Air-to-Air Missile. The AIM-120 had a history of teething troubles and government opposition throughout the 1980s. Despite its early development nearly coming to a halt because it was difficult to perfect (it was technically years ahead of its time), the AIM-120 finally turned out to be one of the most capable weapons available to US air forces. It provides F-15 and F-16 pilots with a missile that has a flexibility and strike capability comparable to that of the F-14's Phoenix.

Navy Phoenix

A missile developed specifically for one type of aircraft is relatively unusual, but the US Navy's F-14

LEFT: Fuselage recesses have enabled the AIM-7 Sparrow and other missiles to be carried by Navy aircraft, thus freeing wing pylons for fuel tanks and ECM pods.

ABOVE: An AIM-54C Phoenix missile undergoes its final visual inspection and cleaning before delivery to the US Navy.

LEFT: Sailors from the ordnance department prepare to load an AIM-54C Phoenix missile onto the wing of an F-14 Tomcat on the flight deck of the USS *Independence*.

Tomcat was designed as are all modern combat aircraft, as an integrated weapons system. Matched with the Hughes AIM-54 Phoenix, the Tomcat was fitted with a large and heavy AAM (nicknamed the "buffalo" for that reason) with a potent and effective "fire and forget" punch over a 100-nm (1825-km) range. The Phoenix has an ability to take out multiple targets, but at a million dollars a shot it became a "last resort" weapon for the fleet's primary fighter which can accommodate up to six. Economies adversely effected upgrades of the F-14, and Navy pilots are encouraged to use an AIM-9 or AIM-120 for their opening shots, rather than a Phoenix.

ABOVE: An AGM-88A HARM high-speed antiradiation missile mounted on a USAF F-4G Wild Weasel aircraft.

RIGHT, TOP: The Standoff Land Attack Missile (SLAM), undergoing a fitting check on an F/A-18 Hornet.

RIGHT, BOTTOM: An F/A -18 Hornet launching a SLAM. The missile shows the tendency of modern air ordnance to get larger but more capable than older weapons.

Antiradiation Missiles

The Vietnam War also initiated the development of another highly significant family of missiles, those designed specifically to destroy hostile radars. Turning the radars' own emissions against them by detecting and locking onto the energy beam, the AGM-45 Shrike and the larger AGM-88 HARM were effective enough. However, the enemy radar had to be transmitting in order for the weapon to home onto it. Operators soon worked out that shutting down their gun or missile fire control sets, even for short periods, could prevent the destruction of their sites. As a counter to a numerically strong Russian-derived ground defense, the larger and more powerful Standard ARM made its debut in Vietnam.

Currently there is an AGM-88C broadband antiradiation missile, which can duplicate all the functions of an aircraft RWR system, store reprogrammable data in an onboard threat library, and select the specific threat for attack.

Air-to-Surface Missiles

US Naval units, at least in terms of non-carrier surface ships, have been in action in recent wars far less than have aircraft, so the deployment of surface-to-air or surface-to-surface missiles has been modest. The AGM-84A/D Harpoon is a large and versatile air-to-surface missile that can also be deployed by ASW helicopters or land-based aircraft. In its latest form the Harpoon is known as the AGM-84E Standoff Land Attack Missile (SLAM), and is carried by the F/A-18 Hornet.

US NAVY
AGM-84-SLAM

Rocket pods

The very widely used 2.75-in (70mm) folding fin aircraft rocket packed in a convenient pod has been adapted to a range of helicopters and light attack aircraft. American helicopters invariably include a 19-round pod on each fuselage stub wing. Earlier versions were augmented by the Hydra pod, which also contains 2.75-in (70mm) rockets. A larger weapon than other air-to-ground rockets, the 5-in (12.7mm) LAU-97 (Zuni) is packed into a four round tube. Widely adopted by the Navy, the Zuni remains a tri-service weapon.

Antitank missiles

AGM-65 Maverick and AGM-114 Hellfire antitank missiles have proven to be devastatingly effective when used with USAF A-10 Thunderbolt II and Apache helicopters. During the Gulf War, Warthog, or A-10, pilots fired around 5,000 Maverick missiles and claimed a successful hit rate of 80 to 90 percent. The score included 987 of the Iraqi tanks that had appeared so potentially deadly before hostilities commenced.

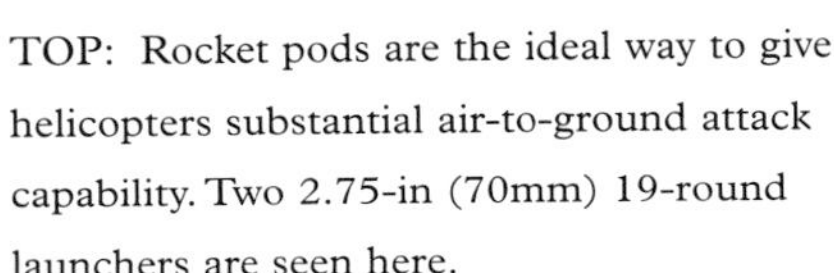

TOP: Rocket pods are the ideal way to give helicopters substantial air-to-ground attack capability. Two 2.75-in (70mm) 19-round launchers are seen here.

ABOVE: A Maverick missile with an infrared seeker, mounted on an F-4 Phantom, receives final checkout prior to being flown to Europe for captive flight tests.

LEFT: Airmen inspect the guidance system assembly on a laser-guided GBU-16 bomb on board the aircraft carrier USS *Nimitz*.

ABOVE, RIGHT: A GBU-24 laser-guided bomb is attached to an F-15 Eagle at Aviano Air Base, Italy.

Bombs

A variety of nuclear bombs in various configurations and different yields were developed for delivery by numerous US combat aircraft, both tactical and strategic, during the Cold War years. Bomb designations include the B-28, B-51, B-61, B-83, and B-93. Today the US air forces rely mainly on an array of free-fall and guided bombs for "force projection" operations. Many of these bombs have now been proven in action. Revising the force structure has led to economies and mission profiles are carefully tailored to minimize costs, if a cheaper weapon is as effective as a prohibitively expensive one, the former is now be the first choice.

A system of steering free-falling aerial bombs onto their target was initiated during the latter stages of the Vietnam War with the Paveway series of "smart" bombs. Utilizing laser technology, GBU-24, -27, and -28 (in various weights) can in a matter of minutes have seeker heads attached to their nose cones and

LEFT: A GBU-15 bomb is prepared before loading onto a Marine F/A-18 Hornet at Aviano Air Base, Italy for a mission over Bosnia Herzegovina.

ABOVE: An F-16 displayed with its total war load. Weapons may be carried in various combinations depending on the mission requirements.

LEFT: Time exposure view of a 2,000lb (907kg) bomb, fitted with a Paveway I guidance unit, about to demolish a truck on a US target range during firing trials.

ABOVE, RIGHT: Laser technology has turned "dumb" bombs into "smart" weapons. Used in conjunction with a designator pod (center), laser-seeker heads give bombs a much greater guarantee of hits than previously.

RIGHT: The "Big Eye" bomb is an aircraft delivered binary chemical bomb. It generates a persistent nerve agent from two non-toxic chemicals, which are shipped and stored separately prior to use.

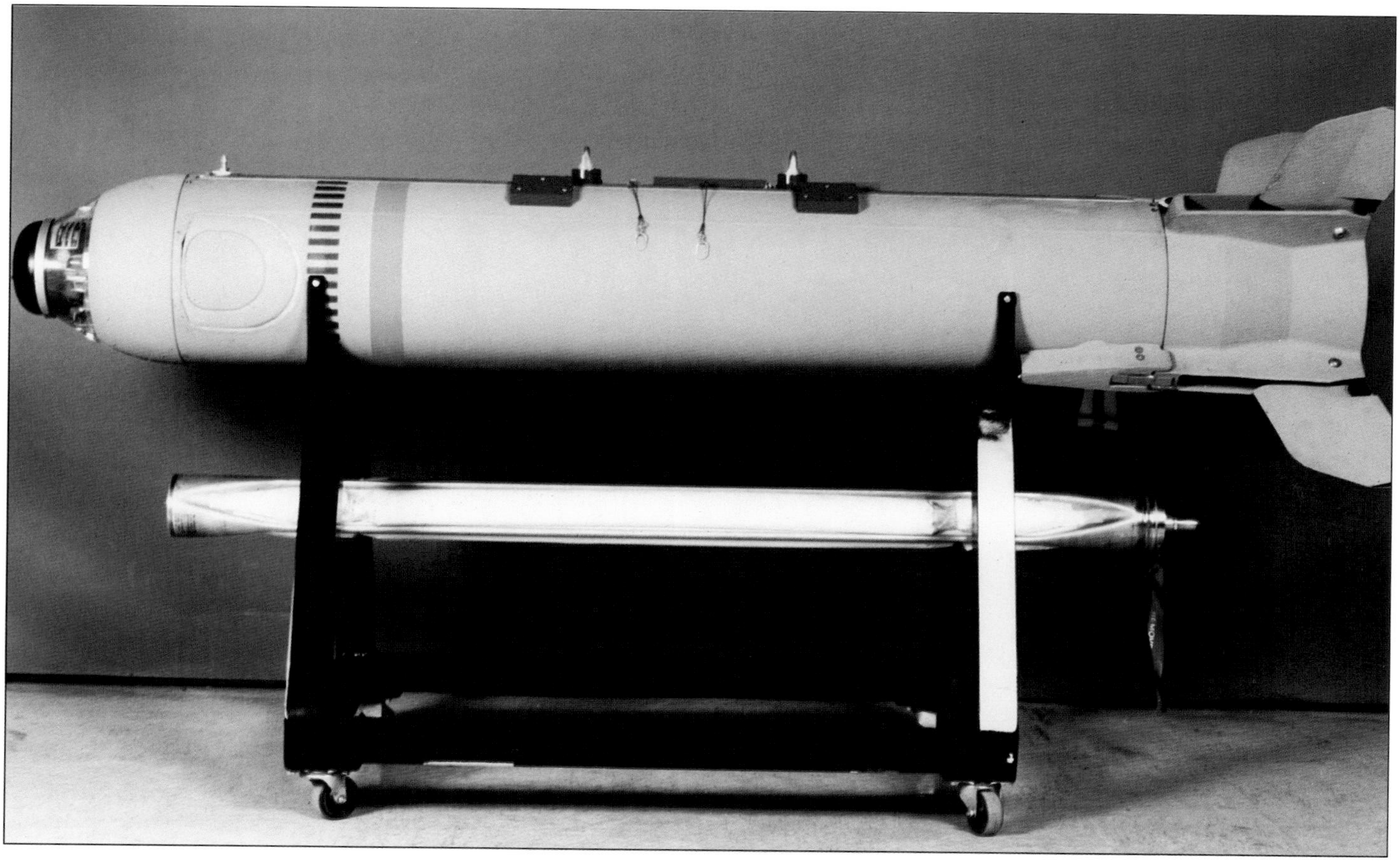

be transformed from humble "dumb" bombs into "smart" munition. Radar and laser guidance has meant a far higher accuracy ratio of launchings to hits than hitherto, although even smart bomb guidance is not totally foolproof. The US is however working toward making precision-guided munitions totally effective.

Cluster Bombs

CBU-59 Rockeye II is the primary US cluster bomb, an air-burst weapon with a streamlined casing designed to split apart just above the ground and spew hundreds of bomblets over a wide area. In the antipersonnel role the effects of such bombs can be devastating. Various other cluster bomb types operating on the same principle, are in the US arsenal. They include the CBU-71 and CBU-71A, which are AP incendiary and antipersonnel types, and have time delay fusing.

RIGHT: Airmen guide a cart of cluster bombs into the staging area for munitions on the flight deck of the USS *Independence* while the ship operates in the Persian Gulf.

BELOW: Rockeye Mk. 20 cluster bombs are designed to split open well clear of the carrier aircraft, which in this case is an A-7 Corsair II, now phased out of USAF inventory.

RIGHT: BLU-109 penetrating bombs, Mk. 84 general purpose bombs, AGM-65 Maverick, AIM-7 Sparrow and AIM-9 Sidewinder missiles are pre-positioned for quick loading onto aircraft.

BELOW, RIGHT: Close-up view of the 1.18in (30-mm) GAU-8A Avenger cannon installed in an A-10 Warthog.

Special Bombs

The CBU-28 Deep Throat bunker-buster is a 4,700lb (2,132kg) penetrator bomb designed specifically to rip apart strongholds buried many feet under ground. It was first used in the closing stages of the Gulf War and in Afghanistan, as the successor to Big Mother, alias the M-121/B-11. Making its debut in Vietnam where it was used to create instant landing pads in deep jungle for helicopters, this 10,000lb (4,536kg) weapon was followed by the 15,000lb (6,804kg) BLU-82 and later the higher tech BLU-109 weighing only 2,000lb (907kg), but with similar characteristics.

The USAF's current inventory includes ample supplies of the 4,700lb (2,132kg) GBU-37B, a bunker-buster that can penetrate three to four layers of 12ft (3.66m) thick reinforced concrete, when released from 45,000ft (13,716m). A sensor in the tail detects how many floors have been penetrated and a signal from the aircraft mission commander then detonates the bomb.

Guns

Slower to adopt cannon as standard aircraft armament than some other countries, the USAF specified 0.79-in (20mm) cannon for the Century series of jet fighters then progressed rapidly to fitting multibarrel weapons to such types as the F-4 and F-105 for Vietnam combat.

Ever larger cannon have been developed for specific aircraft, although the longevity of the 1.2-in (30mm) M61A1 Vulcan, which is also to equip the next generation of fighters (in M61A2 form), marks this weapon out as a standard setter for US aircraft guns designed around the revolver principle. In scaled up form is the 1,350 round General Electric GAU-8 Avenger 1.2-in (30mm) cannon with seven revolving barrels designed for and fitted to the A-10.

The Marines have opted for a weapon using a 25 x 5.4-in (137mm) cartridge (a size suitable for

ABOVE: Longer overall than a small family car, the A-10's Avenger cannon appears to have had the aircraft built around it .

BELOW: GEPOD 30 lightweight 30mm gun pod is shown on body centerline mount on a camouflaged Air Force F4-E Aircraft. The GEPOD 30 fires the family of GAU-8/A ammunition.

ABOVE: A cloud of smoke confirms that an AH-64 pilot has opened fire with his M-230 chain gun during an operational test.

NATO armament compatibility) for the Harrier, known as the GAU-12 Equalizer.

Although the exercise can be expensive, the US has developed several guns for specific aircraft and along with the A-10, the AH-64 Apache has the M-230 chain gun, an externally powered weapon with 625rpg. Using a short 30 x 100lb cartridge, the gun has NATO compatability.

Torpedoes

As the submarine operations of a post-Cold War Soviet Navy represent a much reduced threat to peace, and there is a general lack of surface operations by elements hostile to US forces, the upgrading of torpedoes has a lower priority than it did previously. The Mks. 46 and 50 Barracuda are current developments of the standard ASW aerial torpedoes and these are usually launched by helicopters.

ABOVE: A Mk. 46 torpedo being carried by a Sea King ASW helicopter. With the end of the Cold War the seaborne threat to Allied seaborne forces by conventional navies is much lower than it was.

333
HAND
BRAKE
MAX TOW
20 MPH

Joint Service weapons

Among the largest of the US weapons programs is the integration of a range of munitions into "packages" that can be delivered en masse by long range bombers, such as the B-1 and B-2. For these operations the aircraft are fitted with special Combined Effects Munition Rotary Launchers and Advanced Applications Rotary Launchers. Among the advanced weapons they accommodate are the GNM-137 Triple Service Standoff Attack Missile (TSSAM), the Raytheon AGM-154A, GBU-37B Joint Direct Attack Munition (JDAM), and the JSOW—Joint Standoff Weapon.

LEFT: USAF weapons specialists setting a hoist to the correct weight for moving missiles and bombs into position for loading onto a B-1. Until armed, ordnance can be quite delicate and prone to accidental damage.

LAND WEAPONS

The United States Army is, quite simply, the most powerful army on earth. Financed by the world's largest economy, its sophisticated weaponry, trained personnel, and unified vision ensure that it will remain so in the future. It has at its disposal weapons that can eradicate any conceivable enemy, the will and the people to use that weaponry, and the checks and balances of a democratic system of government to ensure that these forces are used properly. Without that proper use of US forces in two world wars and many postwar conflicts, it is doubtful that as much of the world would be free today.

It was all very different on 14 June 1775 – over a year before the Declaration of Independence – when the US Army was born. The fledgling army very quickly had to prove its worth when it was catapulted into the eight-year Revolutionary War against Great Britain. Celebrating its 225th birthday with the new millennium, the US Army has had to struggle against many foes, internal and external, since winning independence for the nation. It has preserved the Union through four years of bitter conflict in the Civil War; it has defended the United States against external threats—from the "second war of independence" with Great Britain in 1812 through the battles against Nazi totalitarianism, Japanese imperialism, and world communism; and it has struck out against world terrorism.

Today the US Army continues to support democracy all over the world: from the home front, attacked in such a cowardly way on September 11, 2001, to Korea where it defends that country against the communists, and with peacekeeping missions in such locations as Haiti, Bosnia, Kosovo, and East Timor. It works closely with the Drug Enforcement Agency, the US Customs Service, and foreign agencies to halt the flow of illicit drugs into the United States. But the US Army does not simply see its role as an armed force. It has aided victims of floods, earthquakes, hurricanes, war, famine, oil spills, forest fires, and other natural and man-made disasters.

RIGHT: Four men comprise a fire team—team leader, rifleman, grenadier, and automatic rifleman. These men are from the 82nd Airborne, a light infantry division designed to go anywhere on short notice. Parachutes are only a way of getting to work—once on the ground, they operate like any infantry unit.

The Army Vision

On October 12, 1999, as the Chief of Staff of the US Army, General Eric K Shinseki unveiled "The Army Vision"—a blueprint showing how the army would transform to meet the requirements of the new millennium. Its basic tenets were that the US Army should "remain the most respected Army in the world and the most feared ground force to those who would threaten the interests of the United States." To do this the US Army would have to undergo a strategic transformation—losing its cold war structure and appearance to prepare for what would come in the 21st century.

The army identified this transformation as being more than just a technological change but a change to a more agile, versatile, and adaptive force—the Objective Force whose mission would be "a combat capable brigade anywhere in the world in 96 hours; a division on the ground in 120 hours; five divisions on the ground in theater in 30 days."

The Army Vision identifies that soldiers – not equipment – are the army's most important asset and that it must inspire its soldiers to have the strength, the confidence, and the will to fight and win anywhere, anytime. It holds that readiness is the key to versatility. "The Army has a non-negotiable contract with the people of America to fight and win our Nation's wars. We must maintain near-term training and readiness to ensure that we are prepared at all times to carry out our obligations." But more than that, readiness means training its forces to ensure that soldiers are not put in harm's way without the knowledge and means to fulfill their mission.

BELOW: A rifle platoon usually has four squads of nine men each, plus machine gunners, an aid man, a platoon sergeant, and leader. This HHC platoon has twice that with the addition of supporting specialists.

The US Army Soldier

Today adaptation to the latest technology is part of life in the army. New threats need new weapons to combat them and a new mindset to use them effectively in the new tactical scenarios that appear on the battlefield. But while the tasks of today's soldier are often very different than hitherto, today's infantryman—the basic component of any army since time immemorial—isn't all that different from his military ancestors. He tends to be rather young, lean, and tough. If he's been in combat for a while, he will be dirty and smelly—and if he's been in particularly bad combat, he may smell really bad. He is profane and can swear as well as any of his forefathers.

Although some of the weapons and equipment would seem very exotic to a soldier of the Civil War or the two world wars, the basics really haven't changed. The modern soldier's rifle will shoot faster, but its effective range is about the same as that of the Civil War infantryman, about 328 yards (300m), no matter what the official specifications say.

The modern infantryman's rucksack is made of nylon and aluminum, but he carries about the same combat load as an infantryman of the Revolution – typically around 60lb (27.2kg) – and sometimes a lot more. The modern infantryman will sometimes ride into the combat zone in a helicopter, armored personnel carrier, or truck, but he is just as adept at walking 30 miles (48.3km) in a day, if he has to, just as the GIs and Yanks and Rebs did long ago.

However, there have been changes, of course. Today's soldier is in extremely good health and

BELOW: A company commander from 3d Battalion, 7th Infantry, 7th Infantry Division (Light) (3/7/7ID) "gets on the horn" to his deployed platoons with a PRC-77. A radio man provides security for the CO.

ABOVE, LEFT: A soldier uses a Humvee to conduct a morning patrol around the perimeter of an Army base camp in the Kuwaiti desert.

LEFT: A pressure washing system is used to decontaminate an M3 Bradley. The decontamination is part of a chemical training exercise conducted by the Army.

ABOVE: These US Army soldiers are attached to the United Nations Command Security Battalion. They are discussing the next maneuver during a regular patrol of the Demilitarized Zone in the Republic of Korea in 1998.

RIGHT: A soldier operates the throttle of his Bridge Erection Boat during a bridge building training exercise on the Imjin River in the Republic of Korea.

condition—far better than soldiers of the past. He is, statistically, stronger, and better educated, than soldiers of even the recent past. He is a professional, too, rather than a conscript; he wears the uniform by choice and commitment. If he fails to perform to an extremely high standard, his punishment is to be kicked out, back into civil society. That is quite a change from the old conscript Army.

But the real combat soldier shares many things with his military ancestors. Once he has finished training and reached his unit his motivation has almost nothing to do with conventional notions of patriotism and flag-waving, but it does have a lot to do with a sense of honor—an infantryman lives and dies as part of his fire team, squad, platoon, and company. More than anything, he will risk his life to play his role in the bloody little drama; he fears missing his cues and forgetting his lines as much as the slings and arrows of the enemy who serve as critics.

Today's soldiers – male or female – are identified not just by rank but by their Military Occupation Speciality (MOS). There are 212 of these falling into nine categories: Administrative Services, Electronic Maintenance, Engineering and Construction, Health Care, Intelligence and Electronic Communications, Mechanical Maintenance, Media, Public and Civil Affairs, Transportation and Supply Services, and Combat Operations. Of these 212 MOSs there are 30 in Combat Operations involving reconnaissance, security, and other aspects of both offensive and defensive combat situations. These can be further broken down (see following page).

BELOW: A fireteam, this time from the 7th ID. All members of the 7th ID have a piece of camouflage netting attached to their Kevlar helmets giving them a shaggy appearance they have nicknamed the "Tina Turner" look.

Air Defense Artillery: Patriot Missile System Enhanced Operator/Maintainer; Early Warning System Operator; Man Portable Air Defense System Crewmember; Bradley Linebacker Crewmember; Patriot Launching Station Enhanced Operator/Maintainer.

Armor: Cavalry Scout; Armor Crewman.

Aviation Operations: Air Traffic Control Operator; Aviation Operations Specialist.

Combat Engineering: Combat Engineer; Bridge Crewmember.

Field Artillery: Cannon Crewmember; Tactical Automated Fire Control Specialist; Field Artillery Automated Tactical Data Systems Specialist; Cannon Fire Direction Specialist; Fire Support Specialist; Multiple Launch Rocket System Crewmember; Multiple Launch Rocket System Automated Tactical Data Systems Specialist; Field Artillery Firefinder Radar Operator; Field Artillery Surveyor; Field Artillery Meteorological Crewman.

Infantry: Infantryman; Indirect Fire Infantryman; Heavy Anti-armor Weapons Infantryman; Mechanized Infantryman.

Special Forces: Special Operations Weapons Sergeant; Special Operations Engineer; Special Operations Medical Sergeant; Special Operations Communications Sergeant.

The equipment used by these MOSs is covered later.

Organisation—Units and Locations

As you might expect, the US Army has a complex structure that runs from the president down to the men on the ground.

It is the Secretary of the Army (Thomas E White was confirmed the 18th Secretary of the Army on May 31, 2001) who has statutory responsibility for all matters relating to army manpower, personnel, reserve affairs, installations, environmental issues, weapons systems and equipment acquisition, communications,

LEFT: Despite all the aircraft, missiles, ships, tanks, and other combat systems used by the US armed forces, the real ultimate weapon remains something called an "Eleven Bravo," the uncommon infantry foot soldier. This soldier is carrying an M16A1 with M203 attached.

and financial management. His department has an annual budget of nearly $82 billion.

The Secretary of the Army is at the top of a team of just over one million divided into: the Active Component (AC), the Reserve Component (RC) – made up of the Army Reserve National Guard (ARNG) and US Army Reserve (USAR) soldiers – and 220,000 civilian employees. The modernization plan in force calls for an AC with an end strength of approximately 480,000 soldiers; a RC with an end strength of approximately 555,000 soldiers (350,000 ARNG and 205,000 USAR), and a civilian workforce of approximately 215,000 personnel.

The Headquarters, Department of the Army (HQDA) is the executive part of the Department of the Army at the seat of Government. HQDA is composed of the Office of the Secretary of the Army, the Office of the Chief of Staff, Army, the Army Staff, and other staff support agencies not just in Washington DC metropolitan area, but in other dispersed locations.

The most senior man is the Chief of Staff, United States Army—General Eric K Shinseki assumed duties as the 34th incumbent on 22 June 1999.

In 2002, the US Army is organized into the following commands:

US Army Europe (USAREUR), Germany.
US Army Forces Command (FORSCOM), GA, United States.
US Army Materiel Command (AMC), VA, United States.
US Army Training and Doctrine Command (TRADOC), VA, United States.
Eighth US Army (EUSA), Korea.
US Army Corps of Engineers (USACE), DC, United States.
US Army Medical Command (MEDCOM), TX, United States.
US Army Pacific Command (USARPAC), HI, United States.
US Army Space and Missile Defense Command (SMDC), VA, United States.
US Army Special Operations Command (USASOC), NC, United States.
Military Traffic Management Command (MTMC) VA, United States.
US Army Military District of Washington DC (MDW), United States.

ABOVE: This soldier carries an M249 SAW.

LEFT: The name, "Eleven Bravo" is derived from the MOS specification, MOS-11B, meaning an Infantryman. His duties are defined as: "[An infantryman] supervises, leads, or serves as a member of an infantry activity that employs individual or crew served weapons in support of offensive and defensive combat operations."

US Army South (USARSO), Puerto Rico.
US Army Intelligence and Security Command (INSCOM), VA, United States.
US Army Criminal Investigation Command (CID) VA, United States.

The military forces are divided into four corps (I Corps, Fort Lewis, Washington; III Corps, Fort Hood, Texas; V Corps, Heidelberg, Germany; XVIII Airborne Corps, Fort Bragg, North Carolina), and a number of smaller units. Of these there are 12 main AC divisions. The Secretary of the Army is also responsible for over 15 million acres of land all over the US.

Weapons and Equipment

History

The Civil War forced warfare into the Industrial Age. Railways took troops, equipment, and provisions to the front—railway lines and bridges became significant military assets and required defending and supporting. Communications were improved by both the railways and by the telegraph. On the battlefield almost every weapon saw development—the Minie Ball extended effective rifle range to 600 yards (549m). This, in turn, rendered mass infantry advances badly exposed, and Civil War armies started to make more use of trenches, forts, and redoubts. Artillery – the greatest of all battlefield killers today – saw major range increases. These technological advances gained pace as the 19th century continued. The Spanish-American War saw breech-loading repeating rifles as standard issue, and an early version of rapid-firing machinegun, the Gatling Gun, was available as well.

World War I introduced and World War II perfected mechanized alternatives to trench warfare. This led to fast-moving wars where land, air, and sea forces were integrated. There were further improvements to artillery, the arrival and development of the tank, the first multiple rocket launchers, radio for communication; fighter, bomber, and transport aircraft; and paratroops. The US armed forces that entered the Korean War were second to none.

The Korean War saw some improvements in equipment and the introduction of at least one revolutionary item, the helicopter. By the time that US servicemen entered the Vietnam War the helicopter

ABOVE: This soldier, with an M16A2 and a round for the Dragon antitank system on his back, is a Heavy Antiarmor Weapons Infantryman—a MOS-11H "Eleven Hotel". He "as a member of a crew-served weapon squad … Assaults and destroys enemy tanks and armor vehicles, emplacements, weapons, and personnel with heavy anti-armor weapons."

RIGHT and BELOW, RIGHT: An "Eleven Mike"—a mechanized infantryman who "leads, supervises, and serves as a member of a fighting vehicle unit ... Operates both mounted and dismounted to close with and destroy the enemy."

had come into its own—so much so that airmobile units would replace many paratroops. It also contributed materially to improved survival rates of servicemen: medical evacuation (casevac) by helicopter saved thousands of lives.

The successful prosecution of the war with Iraq saw US forces using weapons that would have been classed as science fiction for most of the 20th century—laser-guided ordnance; missile antiaircraft artillery; computer-driven information management, target acquisition, and guidance systems; and low-light capabilities. The Iraqi forces—adequately organized, equipped with Soviet weaponry, and well-versed in the art of war in the desert—were simply blown away. Operations "Desert Shield" and "Desert Storm" saw the forces put in place, the reduction of Iraqi assets by careful, surgical air strikes, and finally a devastatingly brief land campaign.

But the armed forces could not sit back on their heels and congratulate themselves for long. To keep its position as "top dog," the US Army needed to ensure successors to the M1A1 Abrams, Bradley infantry fighting vehicle, Apache attack helicopter, the high-volume, Multiple Launch Rocket System, and Patriot missile. As well as equipment improvements, the army had to ensure the continued high achievement levels by soldiers and their leaders in the demanding world of the high-tech battlefield, thus requiring more skill and initiative than ever from junior officers and NCOs. Now, as always, the success of the soldier is the truest possible measure of the success of the Army. By guaranteeing that soldier the most advanced technology, suitable doctrine, and ample resources available, the United States Army has always sought to accomplish its mission with a minimum loss of life.

Modernization

The goal of the US Army is to remain the top land warfighting force in the world, capable of successfully conducting two nearly simultaneous major theater wars and a wide range of other operations, such as peace enforcement, disaster relief, or humanitarian assistance.

Paul J Kern, Lieutenant General, GS, Military Deputy to the Assistant Secretary of the Army (Acquisition, Logistics, and Technology) sets out the requirements and goals in the US Army's *Weapon Systems Handbook*:

"At the present time … Army forces are not optimally designed and organized … For the 21st Century, the Army envisions a strategically responsive force that is dominant across the entire spectrum of operations and is responsive, deployable, agile, versatile, lethal, survivable, and sustainable. The requirements for greater lethality, survivability, and deployability across the entire force, resulting in greater versatility and agility for full-spectrum operations, point to the need for fundamental transformation and a new vision."

Much of the information on the weapons outlined in this section is based on the *Weapon Systems Handbook* and shows the army's continued determination to find and use the best possible weapons. The selection of weapons mentioned here is not comprehensive, but provides a flavor of what the US Army uses today and intends to use tomorrow.

M1A1/M1A2 Abrams Main Battle Tank

The US Army's main battle tank, the M1A1, has proved itself in action against the Iraqis. Its 4.73-in main gun, 1,500hp turbine engine, and special armor make it a formidable weapon. Modification and update programs include the M1A1D modification scheduled for 1,535 M1A1s (improved computer and a targeting capabilities) and the M1A2 System Enhancement Program that will see 547 Abrams considerably upgraded. A new engine program—the Abrams Integrated Management Overhaul Program is also underway.

The Abrams' 4.73-in (120mm) gun has the most advanced and lethal tank ammunition in the world. Two types of ammunition can be fired from the can-

RIGHT: The foundation of the infantry, the foot soldier, is a rifleman, grenadier, or machine-gunner with about 20 weeks of initial training plus more training within his unit. He may wear the wings of a paratrooper (as here), a Ranger's tab and black beret, or an Air Assault badge. But he is still fundamentally an infantryman who closes with the enemy and defeats him face-to-face.

non: the M829 family of kinetic energy projectiles that use depleted uranium (DU) hard-rod penetrators, and multipurpose ammunition that uses high explosive, shaped-charge warheads to provide blast, armor penetration, and fragmentation effects. The XM1007 Tank Extended Range Munition-Kinetic Energy (TERM-KE) is planned to be a soft-launch, rocket-boosted, terminally-guided, kinetic-energy munition. The XM1028 Canister Cartridge will provide antipersonnel capability at short ranges.

Wolverine Bridgelayer

Designed to provide the heavy brigade combat team with bridgelayer with a gap-crossing capability of up to 26.25 yards (24m), the Wolverine launcher is

RIGHT: Soldier is shown carrying an M60 machinegun.

BELOW: A M-1A1 main battle tank shown in the field. Its 4.8-in (120mm) main gun, 1,500hp turbine engine, and special armor make it a formidable weapon.

ABOVE: Two M1A1 main battle tanks sit in defensive positions as they prepare to engage targets on Range 2 of the Al Hamra Training Area in the United Arab Emirates.

LEFT: US Army 1st Armored Division M1A1 main battle tanks convoy to the Glamoc Ranges in Bosnia and Herzegovina.

ABOVE, RIGHT: A US Army M1A1 main battle tank is equipped with a mine plow which is designed to push mines out of the tank's path, clearing a lane for other vehicles to follow.

RIGHT: A remote-controlled Panther armored mine clearing vehicle leads a column of armored vehicles down a road near McGovern Base in Bosnia and Herzegovina during Operation "Joint Endeavor." The Panther, based on a modified M60 tank hull, uses metal rollers to set off contact or magnetic mines.

ABOVE, LEFT: The basic form of an infantry platoon is three rifle squads, a weapons squad, plus a small headquarters group. The weapons squad usually has two machinegun, antiarmor missile or mortar teams of two men, a gunner and assistant. Headquarters includes the platoon leader, a platoon sergeant, a radio operator (or RATELO), plus two machinegun teams—a total of one officer and 44 soldiers.

ABOVE: The soldier to the left carries an M16A2 and the man to the right an M249 SAW.

mounted on a M1A2 Abrams and is operated by a two-man crew. The 28.4-yard (26-m) long bridge is launched in five minutes, and retrieved in less than ten minutes. It is a major improvement of the current armored vehicle launched bridge (AVLB) that only minimally supports Abrams.

M88A2 Hercules Armored Recovery Vehicle

Designed to provide a battlefield armored recovery vehicle, the Hercules uses the existing M88A1 chassis but with improvements to its towing, winching, lifting, and braking. The Hercules is the primary recovery support for the Abrams and future heavy systems such as the Grizzly, Wolverine, and heavy self-propelled artillery. It entered into service in 2000 with 1st Cavalry Division.

Armored Security Vehicle

The ASV is a turreted, light-armored, all-wheeled drive vehicle that provides increased ballistic and landmine protection to MPs. It entered service at the end of 2000 and its primary weapons are a 1.58-in (40mm) Mk. 19 grenade machinegun, and an M2 .50cal machinegun. The fully enclosed turret includes a day/night sight for target acquisition. Crew size for the ASV is three, with a jump seat for a fourth soldier. The ASV carries up to 3,360lb (1,524kg) of payload and can be transported by a C-130.

M992 Field Artillery Ammunition Support Vehicle

This fully tracked armored vehicle is designed to accompany artillery weapons—particularly the M109A6 Paladin as an ammunition carrier. It has excellent all-terrain capability and an automated conveyer delivery of ammunition. It has excellent ground mobility for improved battlefield responsiveness and a highly improved survivability that allows extended fire support missions. It carries 90, 6.1-in (155mm) projectiles with 96 propelling charges and 104 fuzes, and three Copperhead projectiles. Its combat loaded weight is 57,500lb (26,082kg).

Bradley M2/M3 Infantry/Cavalry Fighting Vehicles

Modern soldiers don't walk as much as their ancestors, and that means they get to the fight a lot faster and fresher. One very important part of the Army's infantry are the "mechanized" units. They have their own "organic" fighting vehicles – traditionally called "battle taxis" – and their own specialized missions. Traditional infantry is now called "light" infantry, and they have another set of missions and skills.

The current battlefield taxi of choice is the M2 Bradley, a fast, agile, well-armed and armored combination of fighting vehicle and personnel carrier that delivers infantry to critical areas of the battlefield while engaging enemy targets with chain gun, coax, and TOW (Tube-launched, Optically-tracked, Wire-guided)missiles.

The specifications and "school solution" will tell you that seven combat-equipped soldiers will fit in one, but the people who came up with that figure don't seem to have tried it. For most of the troops, the Bradley is pretty comfortable. But there is one seat, right behind the driver, that requires its assigned

ABOVE and LEFT: M2 Bradleys weigh about 25 tons and have a 600hp diesel engine. The primary armament on the M2 is a 1-in (25mm) chain gun. TOW missiles launched from the M2 can out-range an enemy tank by engaging it at 9842ft (3,000m).

passenger to squeeze through a very small and cluttered tunnel on the right side of the turret. It is quite possible for a soldier to get into this seat—but nobody can do it while wearing their LBE and expect to get back out again. The Bradley crews and the infantry who ride in them refer to this seat as the "hell hole." Sometimes a soldier will actually sit in there, but he leaves his LBE and weapon in the main passenger compartment and tries to get it on as he dashes down the ramp, far behind the rest of the men in his squad. Normally, the seat is empty and the squads either fight short-handed or split up the men into multiple Bradleys.

The Bradley was initially designed to help the M1 Abrams MBT fend off potential attacks during a possible world war. It is almost as fast as the Abrams in open terrain and faster when the going gets really rough. Bradleys are often confused with tanks, but they are quite vulnerable to the cannon of even old and obsolete MBTs such as the T-55s and T-72s used by threat nations all over the world. The 4.14-in (105mm) and 4.43-in (120mm) projectiles from these tanks would slice through a Bradley without slowing down—if they ever get a shot at one.

ABOVE and RIGHT: The current "battlefield taxi" of choice is the M2 Bradley. Seven combat-equipped soldiers are meant to fit in one, but this is only possible at a tight squeeze and if one soldier sits in the "hell hole" behind the driver's seat. Usually this seat is left empty and the squads fight short-handed or men are carried in several Bradleys.

BELOW and LEFT: Bradleys mount a M240C co-axial 0.3-in (7.62mm) machinegun with 800 rounds in the ready boxes and another 1,400 stowed.

Bradleys have thin armor only intended to protect against small arms and machinegun fire and the shrapnel from nearby artillery impacts.

Bradleys weigh about 25 tons, less than half the weight of a MBT, thanks to the lighter armor and smaller size. They are propelled by a 600hp diesel engine that will move the M2 along at 45mph (72kmph) or better (although the Army says top speed is only 38mph – 61kmph). With a full tank of 175 USgallons (145 UKgallons)of fuel aboard, a Bradley can travel about 175 miles (281km) under ideal road conditions although that tank will need refilling much sooner when the vehicle operates in tactical conditions.

Primary armament on the M2 is a 1-in (25mm) chain gun optimized for engaging enemy lightly-armored vehicles and "thin-skinned" trucks, but can also engage area targets such as troops in the open, helicopters, and fortified positions. The infantry version of the Bradley, the M2A2 and A3, carry 600

LEFT: The Bradley was initially designed to help the M1 Abrams main battle tank. It is almost as fast as the Abrams in open terrain.

BELOW, LEFT: Bradleys are often confused with tanks, but are quite vulnerable to the cannon of even old and obsolete main battle tanks, such as the T-55 and T-72s.

RIGHT: The main compartment of the Bradley that will carry six soldiers.

BELOW: The driver's compartment of the Bradley.

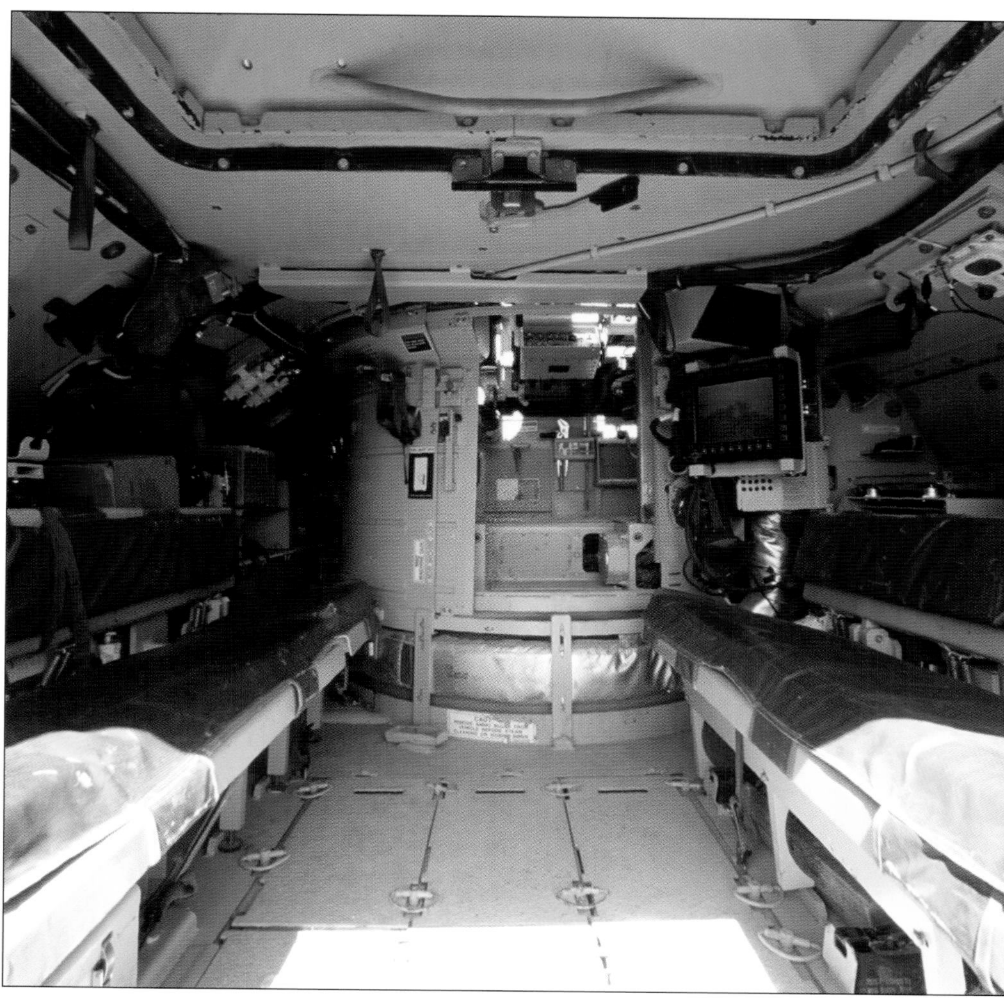

rounds for the chain gun, in two types—high explosive (HE) for trucks, troops, and aircraft, and armor-piercing (AP) for enemy APCs.

Bradleys may not be able to take a hit from a MBT but they can certainly inflict one with TOW missiles. The TOW missile can out-range an enemy tank by engaging it at 3,281 yards (3.000m), beyond the target's weapon's effective range. Although it takes 14 seconds for the missile to get to the target at that range, it is extremely accurate and lethal; the most recent variants of the missile will defeat any modern tank, with or without reactive armor.

For those situations when enemy infantry swarm around your position, Bradleys mount a M240C co-axial 0.3-in (7.62mm) machinegun with 800 rounds in the ready boxes and another 1,400 stowed.

Bradley Fire Support Vehicle (BFIST)

One of the M2/M3 Bradley derivatives, the FSV is designed to provide an integrated Bradley based fire-support platform so that officers can plan, coordinate, execute, and direct timely, accurate, indirect fires. It is planned to upgrade the BFIST to both Bradley M2A2 Operation "Desert Storm"-based improvements (M7 BFIST) and M2A3 variants (A3 BFIST).

M6 Bradley Linebacker Air Defense Vehicle

The Linebacker is the air-defense variant of the Bradley modified by replacing the TOW missile launcher with a four-missile Stinger standard vehicle-mounted launcher.

M707 Striker Fire Support Team Vehicle

The Striker replaces the M981 Fire Support Team Vehicles used by Combat Observation Lasing Teams (COLTs). It operates as an integral part of the brigade reconnaissance team, providing COLT and fire support mission planning and execution. The crew on board Striker locates and designates targets for laser-guided ordnance. It is built on a HMMWV chassis.

BELOW: A Hummer shown here with a TOW antitank missile system mounting.

M998 High Mobility Multipurpose Wheeled Vehicle

One of the Army's big success stories of recent years is the sturdy little vehicle called the High Mobility Multipurpose Wheeled Vehicle, known affectionately as the "Hummer." It has been in the infantry motor pool since 1983 and was a hit from the beginning. Fifteen versions of the basic design have been built, and over 70,000 have been put in service.

The basic Hummer is much bigger than the traditional jeep of old: the basic model weighs about three tons (5,900lb/2,676kg), has a 2,500lb (1,134kg) payload, and has a kind of odd, low, wide stature. It has full time four-wheel drive, independent suspension, and a very reliable 6.5-liter V-8 engine. You can take one up a 60 percent slope or ford a stream five feet deep. The HMMWV's long wheelbase and wide track make it remarkably agile and reasonably comfortable when rattling around the wadis and deserts of the Valley of Death or the Goat Trail at the National Training Center (NTC).

The main body material, is aluminum, one of the factors that make the Hummer so easily air-deployable. They are dropped by parachute or delivered to austere forward airstrips from C-130s. CH-47 heli-

LEFT: The M998 High Mobility Multipurpose Wheeled Vehicle is otherwise known as the Hummer.

BELOW: TOW missile being fired from a Hummer.

copters easily carry two of them as sling loads to inaccessible locations, and a UH-60 can carry one.

It can be configured to become a troop carrier, armament carrier, S250 shelter carrier, ambulance, TOW missile carrier, and a Scout vehicle. The heavy variant, with a payload of 4,400lb (1,996kg), was developed as the prime mover for the light howitzer, towed Vulcan system, and heavier shelter carriers. It is a tri-service program that also provides vehicles to satisfy Marine Corps and Air Force requirements. Company commanders and platoon leaders all have Hummers of their own, complete with driver and stuffed with SINCGARS radios, and with a case of MREs, a water cooler, and field gear during tactical operations. Most infantry soldiers will spend at least some time riding around in one of the versions, and all agree that the ride is better than walking.

M113 Armored Personnel Carrier

Although too slow and vulnerable to play much of a role on the modern battlefield, the old M113 is still part of the inventory and still performing essential missions for the modern infantryman. Bradleys have taken over the battlefield taxi business, but the basic M113 (in a modified version called the M577) provide the foundation for a mechanized infantry battalion's tactical operations center. You will generally find a large coffee pot in one of the M577s clustered together at the TOC, and the others will be home to the fire support officer, the S3 Operations crew, and all the other staff that keep the battalion in business. The M113s that remain in service provide a highly mobile, survivable, and reliable tracked-vehicle platform designed to keep pace with Abrams and Bradley-equipped units. The current list of models include:

- M58 Mechanized Smoke Obscurant System
- M548A1/A3 Cargo Carrier,
- M577A2/A3 Command Post Carrier
- M901A1 Improved TOW Vehicle
- M981 Fire Support Team Vehicle
- M1059/A3 Smoke Generator Carrier
- M1064/A3 Mortar Carrier
- M1068/A3 Standard Integrated Command Post System Carrier, and OPFOR Surrogate Vehicle (OSV).

BELOW: Although it no longer plays much of a role on the modern battlefield, the M901A1 Improved TOW vehicle still forms part of the Army's inventory.

ABOVE: The M901A1 Improved TOW Vehicle (ITV)consists of a standard M113A1 APC with an M27 cupola mounted on the roof.

BELOW: When traveling, the launcher head is retracted level onto the hull top so making the ITV difficult to distinguish from the standard M113A1 series APC.

TOP: The M901A1 Improved TOW provides a highly mobile, survivable, and reliable tracked-vehicle platform.

ABOVE: The M901A1 is designed to keep pace with Abrams and Bradley-equipped units.

RIGHT: Soldiers assigned to C Troop of the 4th Squadron, 7th Cavalry Regiment drive an M113A1 Armored Personnel Carrier to the live fire range at the Korea Training Center, Republic of Korea. Armored units use the range to meet annual, live gunnery training requirements.

2-4-7CAV
C 52
A42

M16A1/A2 Rifle and M4 Carbine

The most common weapon in the whole Army is certainly the M16 rifle and its several variants. The design is almost 50 years old at this point, and has been in US service for 35 years. Dozens of nations around the world also use it, a testament to its excellent design and manufacture.

Most soldiers today love the weapon; it is light, strong, accurate, reliable, and it puts a killing round downrange. But American soldiers haven't always been so fond of it. During the late 1960s, shortly after it was introduced, the propellant used in the ammunition for the weapon was changed and soldiers reported numerous problems with failure to feed and jamming. Those problems have long been solved and today's soldiers seldom have any stoppages with the weapon.

The current basic variants found in infantry units are the M16A2 rifle and M4 carbine. The M16A2 weighs 8.7lb (4kg), is 39in (1m) long, and has a maximum range of 3,937 yards (3,600m). Its maximum effective range is rated at 634 yards (580m)—an extremely optimistic official figure for real-world combat engagements against individual soldiers.

The old A1 version offered a choice of single shots or fully automatic. The predictable result was that in combat during the Vietnam War inexperienced soldiers switched to auto, forgot all their training about fire discipline, and aimed fire, executing an engagement technique known as "spray and pray." Their first rounds might possibly have been in the general vicinity of an enemy soldier but the rest of the 20 or 30 in the magazine almost certainly pruned the trees over the opposing team. These soldiers rapidly found themselves running low on ammunition without having done any damage at all to the Viet Cong or NVA.

When it came time to take another look at the M16, and the A2 went onto the drawing board, the full auto feature was deducted in favor of a three-shot

LEFT: A soldier patrols near a US observation post in Mijak, Kosovo, Serbia. US troops in Mijak regularly patrolled the area in an attempt to prevent shipments of arms from crossing the border into Macedonia.

RIGHT: M16A1 with M203 attached. The A1 uses a special upper hand-guard with the M203. A ramp sight attached to the hand-guard helps put the 1.6-in (40mm) rounds on target but, because of the projectile's steep trajectory, precision fire is difficult to achieve.

ABOVE: Soldier with M16A1 with M203 attached. The A1 version offered a choice of single shots or a fully automatic feature. This automatic feature was changed in favor of a three-shot burst on the A2.

burst. This feature still lets the inexperienced soldier waste a lot of ammunition, but forces him to engage targets with a weapon that is more controllable.

The round fired by the rifle was a radical shift from infantry tradition when it was introduced, too. It is a tiny little bullet, dwarfed by the projectile used with the old and beloved M1 Garand of World War II and Korea and even the 0.3-in (7.62mm) NATO round fired by the M14. But its light weight and small diameter has a couple of virtues that have gradually won over the troops. For one, the soldier can carry a lot more rounds for a given weight—210 are a typical combat load. For another, the bullet comes zipping out of the muzzle at 2,800ft/sec (853m/sec); it is a very flat-shooting round within its normal engagement ranges, and inflicts devastating wounds before the velocity falls off around 219 or 328 yards (200 or 300m) out.

The weapon is capable of firing 800rpm but 12 to 15 is a realistic maximum sustained rate of fire. If a soldier really gets into some deep trouble and has to use that three-shot-burst capability, 90rpm is possible. Thirty-round magazines are standard with the weapon but 20-round versions are sometimes used, and even Rambo has to change them once in a while.

According to the Army, the M16A2 can be used to engage "point" targets out to 634 yards (580m). That's a third of a mile, and at that range an enemy soldier has very little to fear from about 95 percent of riflemen—for the first shot, at least. It takes a very good marksman to hit a man at that range, even if he is just standing still and in the open like an idiot.

The Army says the weapon is useful to 1094 yards (1000m)for "area" targets—that is a gaggle of troops in the open, for example; you may annoy them with your three-shot bursts, and if you are very lucky (and he is not) you might even hit one at that distance, if you fire enough rounds. But killing engagements are typically at 218 yards (200m) and closer – generally a lot closer – and the M16 in its long history and several variants has been in a lot of them.

A lot of soldiers are surrendering their rifles for the lightweight M4 carbine. It is almost the same weapon but has a collapsible stock and shorter barrel making it even lighter than the original. The shorter

ABOVE: An M16A2 uses a small bullet that seems dwarfed in comparison to the old projectile used with the memorable M1 Garand of World War II.

sight radius makes it a little less accurate at long range, but that is seldom a problem. It is much easier to carry when hopping in and out of helicopters, trucks, Bradleys, trench-lines, and enemy bunkers.

M203 Grenade Launcher

Direct fire weapons such as the M16 rifle are excellent for certain kinds of targets but utterly useless for

BELOW: M16A1 and M203 with 1.6-in (40mm) rounds in bandolier. The 203 fires high-explosive, illumination, smoke, flechette, dual-purpose, training, and "beanbag rounds." The training round is only filled with red powder but works well for marking the point of impact.

LEFT: A soldier of Bravo Company, 1st Battalion, 8th Marines, engages the enemy with his M16A2 rifle.

BELOW, LEFT: A soldier uses a M16A2 rifle to maintain his marksmanship qualifications at a range near Handalici, Bosnia, and Herzegovina, during Operation Joint Endeavor.

BELOW: A Mark 19 automatic grenade launcher is fired at the Marine Corps Base in Virginia. This grenade launcher is capable of a maximum range of well over a mile and a maximum effective range of 1750 yards (1600m). It can fire 350rpm but 60rpm is usually the case.

others. During the war in Vietnam and Southeast Asia, infantry soldiers were issued the M79 grenade launcher, a stubby little single shot weapon that fired a 1.58-in (40mm) low velocity round. The M79's high-explosive, smoke, and "bean-bag" rounds proved to be extremely effective against VC and NVA in all sorts of situations. The HE round could be fired into bunkers or at enemy soldiers behind the crest of a hill; the smoke round could provide a bit of screening for an attack or withdrawal; the "bean-bag" round was very effective at temporarily incapacitating an enemy soldier, like a massive punch to the torso, without doing (much) permanent damage—a great way to collect a prisoner for questioning.

Today's grenadier uses a similar weapon, the M203, but his launcher is attached to the same M16A2 used by the riflemen in the squad, and his

ABOVE: A 1st Platoon, Lima Company Marine uses his ski poles to steady his M16A2 rifle equipped with a M203 grenade launcher during part of his training in cold weather survival and arctic warfare.

weapon has a tremendous variety of ammunition available. Among these are HE, dual purpose, several varieties of smoke rounds, several star-cluster signaling rounds, non-lethal projectiles, a "buckshot" projectile, and the really nasty flechette round. This latter sprays several dozen small, heavy, extremely sharp steel darts downrange, any one of which will likely make even Rambo drop his weapon and quit.

The launcher adds 3lb (1.36kg) to the weight of the M16 making the assembly almost 12lb (5.44kg) with a full mag in the rifle. The grenades can be used to engage point targets such as a bunker aperture, a window, fighting position, or vehicle out to 164 yards (150m). For area targets, such as troops in the open, it is used to 383 yards (350) or so. Maximum range is 437 yards(400m).

M240B Medium Machinegun

The M240B is a ground-mounted, gas-operated, crew-served machinegun. This reliable 0.3-in (7.62mm) machinegun delivers a bigger punch than the smaller caliber M249 SAW. It will be issued to infantry, armor, combat engineer, and special force units that require medium support and will replace the M60 series machineguns currently in use.

RIGHT: The M60 machinegun is capable of firing 200rpm and 100rpm of sustained fire, just the kind of weapon needed to initiate an ambush on an enemy platoon.

M60 Machinegun and M249 Squad Automatic Weapon

The M60 sucks up 0.3-in (7.62mm) NATO rounds at a rapid rate—550 rounds cyclic rate, 200 rpm when the bad guys are coming through the wire, and 100rpm sustained. Even 100 rounds of M60 ammunition is a heavy load, and somebody has to carry it. That somebody is every guy in the squad, each of whom gets a box or belt to stuff in his backpack.

But that firepower is just what you need when it comes time to break contact, or when the assault elements are rushing the enemy bunker. It is also just the job when you initiate an ambush on an enemy platoon—you either cut down those 45 NVAor they are going to put you in (so to speak) a "world of hurt."

The M60 has been largely replaced by the M249 Squad Automatic Weapon, known as the SAW. This machinegun is a Belgian design from Fabrique Nationale Manufacturing and has become quite popular—especially with soldiers who used to have to "hump" the "pig" over hill and dale. Complete with bipod and tools, the weapon weighs just over 15lb (6.8kg) empty; a 200-round plastic "battle pack" box magazine adds another 7lb (3.17kg), but that is still far less than an M60 and 200 rounds.

SAWs fire the same 0.22-in (5.56mm) cartridge used by the M16 and can even accept the standard 30-round magazines carried by every rifleman. This allows the SAW gunner to beg, steal, or borrow more ammunition when he runs out, not an option for the M60 gunner. He starts out with 600 rounds for his basic load, though, and it will take him a while to get through it all.

M249s have a cyclic rate of fire of 600rpm but the gunner will have the squad leader screaming at him if he keeps that up for long. Sustained fire is 85rpm or less. The SAW is good for area targets out to 875 to 1,094 yards (800m to1,000m) or against point targets to 656 yards (600m).

ABOVE, RIGHT: Soldiers call the big M60 machinegun the "pig," and if you had to carry one and a basic load of ammunition for a mile or two, you would understand why. Weighing 23lb (10.4kg) when empty, it is a hefty load.

RIGHT: Even 100 rounds of M60 ammunition is a heavy load and each soldier gets a belt or box to stuff in his backpack.

Although it doesn't have a three-shot burst control, the gunner should be able to manage that on his own. With practice, a gunner can squirt three, four, or six rounds downrange, under control and with reasonable accuracy. Long bursts are for the movies—in the real world, the barrel starts to glow cherry red very quickly and the ammunition starts to "cook off" as soon as it chambers, and then the gun is out of control.

During sustained engagements the gunner is very careful to manage his rate of fire, and will swap out barrels quite frequently, allowing one to cool while he heats the other one up with those well-disciplined bursts of carefully aimed fire.

Mk. 19 1.58-in(40mm) Grenade Launcher

An industrial-strength grenade launcher is the Mk. 19, a kind of machinegun for 1.58-in (40mm) projectiles. Although it fires ammunition that appears similar to that used with the M203, the Mk. 19 throws its rounds out much farther with a maximum range of well over a mile and a maximum effective range of 1750yards (1,600m). It is a heavy weapon, weighing 137lb (62kg) in total, so it isn't carried by the foot soldiers. Instead, it is mounted on humvees and trucks, or carried in them and dismounted for use in defensive positions. The Mk. 19's cyclic rate of fire is about 350rpm but 60rpm is tops for the real world and 40rpm the maximum rate of fire for sustained engagements.

One of the rounds fired by this weapon, the M430 HEDP (High Explosive Dual Purpose), will punch through two inches of armor. Fragments from this round and the HE version will kill enemy soldiers within 5.47yards (5m) of impact and probably wound anybody within 16.4 yards (15m).

ABOVE, RIGHT: The Barrett .50cal sniper rifle is testimony to the renewed interest in the Army and Marine Corps in extreme long-range precision shooting. They call it "target interdiction," and with one of these weapons a trained shooter can make first-shot kills at ranges exceeding 1094 yards (1000m). The Barrett weighs 28.5lb (13kg), fires as a semi-automatic, and its magazine holds ten rounds.

RIGHT: M18 smoke grenades are frequently used to signal a position and to obscure.

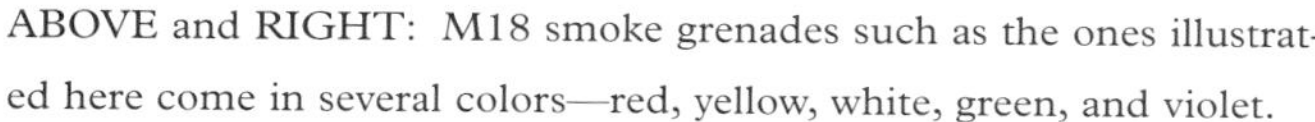

ABOVE and RIGHT: M18 smoke grenades such as the ones illustrated here come in several colors—red, yellow, white, green, and violet.

BELOW: The M67 hand grenade weighs about a pound and is a potent little package. Up to six may be carried by combat infantrymen during operations. Once the pin is removed from the M67 (and NOT with your teeth!) and the "spoon" is released, the soldier has between four and five seconds to take cover before the weapon detonates. This hand grenade once detonated will kill anybody within 16.4ft (5m) and wound most within a range of 50ft (15m).

M2 .50cal Machinegun

Soldiers call this fine old weapon "Ma Duce," and it is an affectionate nickname. The M2 heavy machinegun design goes all the way back to 1923 and is still in the inventory because of its tremendous effectiveness, reliability, and range. Fired single shot, it is so accurate that M2s were used as sniper weapons in Vietnam, making single-shot kills on NVA soldiers at distances up to a mile. But the Ma Duce is normally employed against enemy soldiers in the open, sometimes at great distances, against trucks, light armor, and slow-flying aircraft.

Several types of ammunition are issued: M33 ball and M17 tracer are the most common, mixed at a five-to-one ratio in belts of 100 rounds. Armor-piercing, armor-piercing-incendiary, and even discarding-sabot armor-piercing rounds are also issued, all highly effective against thin-skinned enemy vehicles. Sustained rate of fire is just 40rpm—and that requires regular barrel changes.

A new round, the Mk. 211, combines an delayed explosive charge with an armor-piercing projectile. Instead of exploding on impact, the Mk. 211 projectile is designed to penetrate light armor first, then detonates once inside creating more damage than earlier projectiles.

2.36in (60mm) Mortar and 3.19in (81mm) Mortar

So what do you do when the bad guys are on the far side of a building, berm, hill, in a trench, or hiding behind something solid? Call up the mortars! The three-man mortar squad and their M224 Lightweight 2.36-in Mortar can drop rounds on the opposing team in their holes where no direct-fire weapons can reach them.

The 2.36-in (60mm) mortar is light enough to travel with the infantry wherever they go. Its crew—squad leader, gunner, and ammunition bearer—split its 46.5lb (21kg) up into two loads, the tube and mount forming one and the base-plate the other. The ammo bearer has enough to carry already so the squad leader and gunner will hump the weapon. Once they get the call for fire, the mortar squad can pump out high-explosive, white phosphorus, and illumination rounds, helping the infantry unit with immediate, organic indirect fire support. They can hammer any target from just 76.6 yards (70m) to almost 3828 yards (3,500m).

BELOW: At 128lb (58kg), the M2 and its tripod are carried by vehicles. They are frequently found on mounts attached to M113s (as here), 5-ton trucks, and HWWMVs. An M2 can reach 5905ft (1.8km), or take out a point target 3937ft (1.2km).

ABOVE: The 2.4-in (60mm) mortar is light enough to be taken with the infantry wherever they go. Its 46.5lb (22kg) weight is split into two loads, the tube and mount forming one and the base-plate the other.

The HE round is certainly the most common and is used to kill enemy soldiers and to damage vehicles, structures, and similar unarmored objects. The HE and other rounds have one of two kinds of fuzes installed, one, the M935, that explodes on impact, and the very useful M734 Multioption fuze. The latter version allows the mortar team to set the round to explode about 10ft (3m) above the surface, just above the surface, on impact, or a half-second after impact. The first two options work well against troops in the open or in hasty defensive positions, the delay setting will help defeat troops in prepared positions with over head cover.

Besides the normal high-angle fire typical of mortars, the M224 has the capability of low-angle direct fire. The weapon can be fired with a manual trigger and when the base of the tube is supported by a substantial tree trunk or similar suitable object, the mortar becomes a kind of small howitzer or huge shotgun. Employed in this way, targets as close as 76.6 yards (70m) can be engaged.

In an emergency, 30rpm can be fired for a total of four minutes—but that takes a lot of ammunition, much more than is likely to be available to a squad mortar section in normal combat. During sustained operations, 20rpm is more likely to be the practical maximum that can be obtained.

Although quite heavy at almost 90lb (40kg), the M252 3.19-in (81mm) mortar system is still an essential part of the infantry's bag of tricks. For real hardcore units, the weapon can be broken down into its components—the 35lb (15.8kg) tube, the 25.5lb (11.6kg) baseplate, 26lb (11.8kg) bipod, and 2.5lb (1.1kg) sight—and man-packed off into the weeds where it will provide industrial-strength fire support.

It is accurate to 6,234 yards (5,700m) firing HE, illumination, and smoke rounds at the rate of 15rpm. One illumination round will light up the night with 600,000 candlepower for a minute, revealing any enemy sappers trying to sneak through the wire.

4.73-in(120mm) Mortar

The 4.73-in (120mm) mortar system is a conventional smoothbore, muzzle-loaded mortar system that is a great improvement on the World War II-vintage 4.2-in (107mm) heavy mortar system it replaced. It is employed in towed (M120) and carrier versions (M121) and fires enhanced ammunition.

The Mortar Fire Control System (MFCS) will provide Paladin-like fire control capability that greatly improves mortar lethality, responsiveness, and crew survivability. New infrared illumination ammunition, the first of its kind in the world, provides enhanced nightfighting capability. Other improved munitions include the XM395 Precision Guided Mortar Munition (PGMM) – extended-range precision-guided munition with a strap-down laser detector seeker – and the XM984 Dual Purpose Improved Conventional Munition (DPICM)—extended-range munition that incorporates composites to maximize the number of dual-purpose grenades that can be carried.

Javelin Antitank Missile System

The Javelin is a portable, antiarmor system in service with the US Army and US Marine Corps. Javelin was designed to replace the Dragon. It is highly lethal against tanks with both conventional and reactive armor. The Javelin system weighs 48lb (21.7kg) and has a maximum range in excess of 2,734 yards (2,500m). The key feature of Javelin is the use of fire-and-forget (F&F) technology that enables the gunner to fire and immediately take cover.

BELOW: The M47 Dragon's complete system consists of the launcher, the tracker, and the missile, which is installed in the launcher during final assembly and received by the army in a ready to fire condition.

TOW Antitank Missile System

TOW is designed to defeat tanks and armored vehicles equipped with advanced armors at close ranges with minimal exposure time. A fire-and-forget (F&F) missile system, the intention is to ensure it is given increased range, lethality, and platform survivability shelf life extension efforts.

M47 Dragon multipurpose weapon

A medium-range complement to TOW, this antitank or assault weapon has a range from 65.6 to 1,094 yards (60–1,000m), and a 5.4lb (2.45kg) warhead. In service since 1971, it has been replaced by the more effective Javelin.

TOP: The M47 Dragon is a medium-range, wire-guided, line-of-sight antitank missile weapon capable of defeating armored vehicles, fortified bunkers, concrete gun emplacements, and other hard targets.

ABOVE: The M47 is too heavy to be carried permanently on a soldier's shoulder. In order to use it, a soldier needs to deploy, changing the M16A2 for self defense to an M47 Dragon.

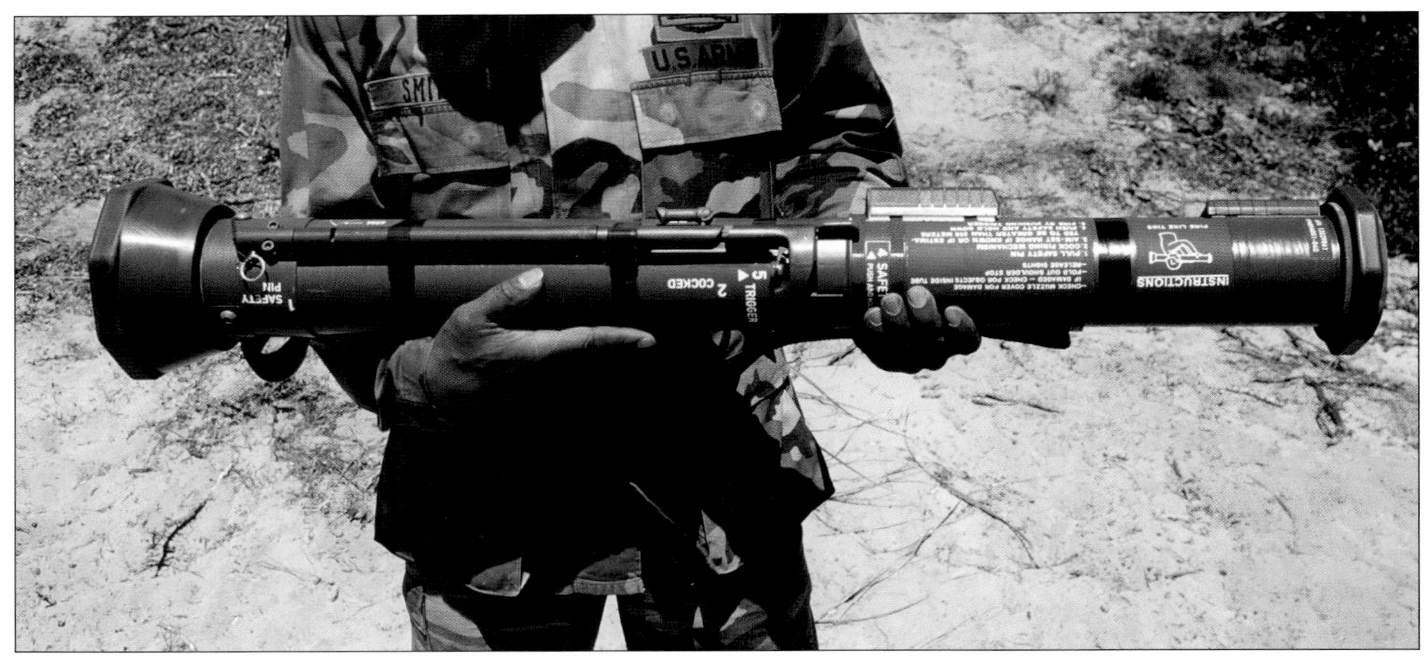

U.S.ARMY
1 SAFETY PIN
2 COCKED
5 TRIGGER
4 SAFE
INSTRUCTIONS

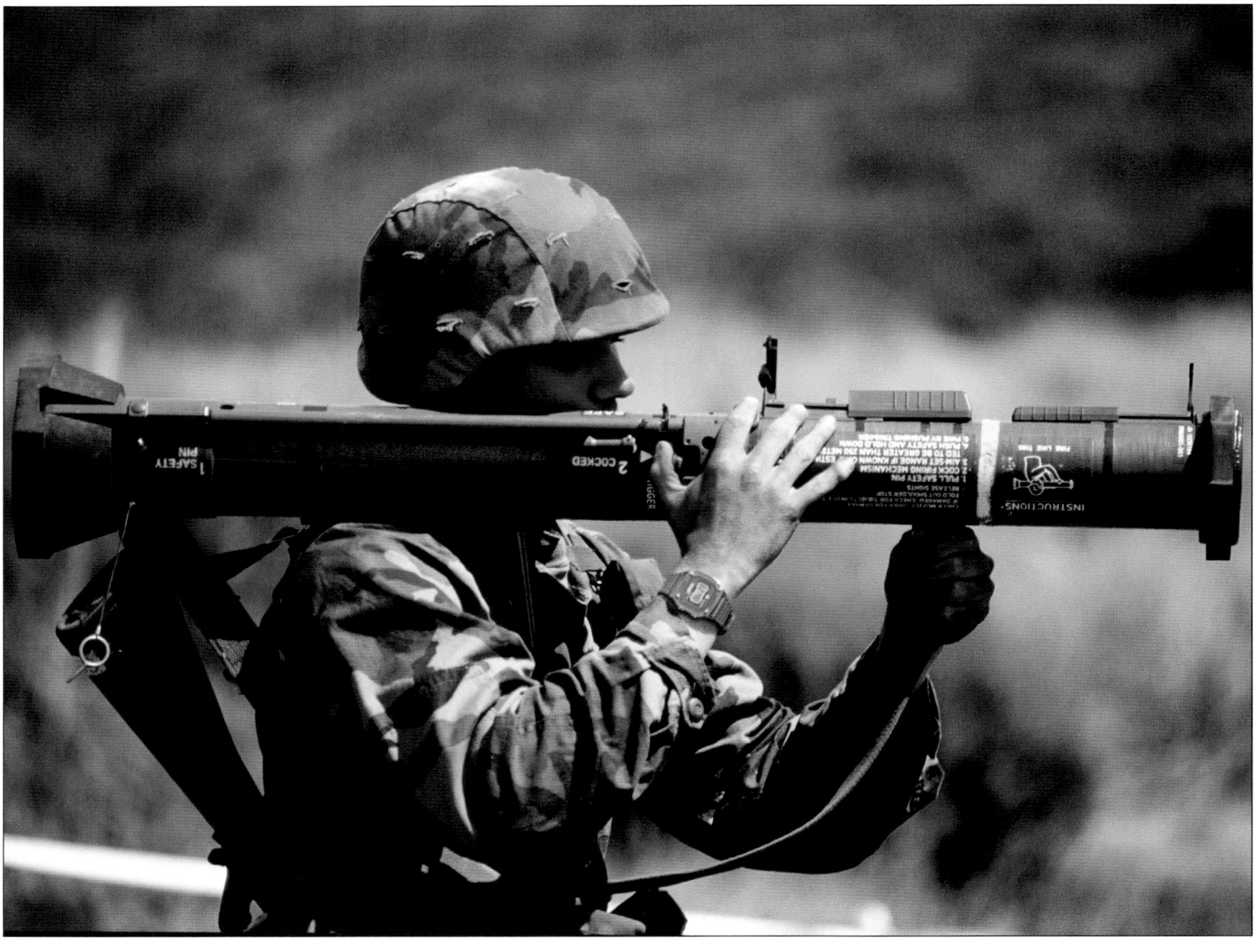
1 SAFETY PIN
2 COCKED
INSTRUCTIONS

LEFT and BELOW, LEFT: The Swedish-designed AT4, weighing is a multipurpose weapon used in the antitank and bunker-buster roles, firing shaped-charge ammunition.

RIGHT: The M72A3 LAW is a lightweight, self-contained, antiarmor weapon consisting of a rocket packed in a launcher. It is is man portable and may be fired from either shoulder.

AT4 Lightweight Multipurpose Assault Weapon

This single-shot throwaway 3.31-in (84mm) antitank rocket was produced to replace the LAW. It entered service in 1989. It has a range of over 328 yards (300m), firing fin-stabilized HE-shaped charge ammunition.

M72 Light Antitank Weapon

Now obsolescent, this is a throwaway antitank system that gave the infantry a useful antiarmor capability.

ABOVE: The launcher on the M72A3, which consists of two tubes, one inside the other, serves as a watertight packing container for the rocket and houses a percussion type firing mechanism that activates the rocket.

ABOVE: Marines launch a Stinger antiaircraft missile at a target aircraft during a live fire exercise. This missile homes in on the heat emitted by aircraft and other targets.

Stinger Antiaircraft Missile System

A short-range air defense missile, Stinger is a fire-and-forget infrared/ultraviolet (IR/UV) missile system and is mounted on a variety of platforms including Avenger, Kiowa Warrior, Special Operation Black Hawks (MH-60), Bradley Linebacker, and the US Marine Corps' Light Amphibious Vehicle—Air Defense. This missile homes in on the heat emitted by aircraft and other targets. Stinger uses an eject motor to propel the missile a safe distance away from the gunner; a flight motor then ignites and propels it to the target.

Avenger Antiaircraft Missile/Gun System

The Avenger system is a lightweight, highly mobile, and transportable surface-to-air missile/gun weapon system mounted on an M998 HMMWV. It has a two-man crew and can operate during the day or night and in clear or adverse weather conditions. The system incorporates a rotating turret and standard vehicle-mounted launchers which support and launch multiple Stinger missiles. Avenger can be operated remotely up to 54.7 yards (50m) from the fire unit and can shoot on the move.

BELOW: An Avenger Gunner from the 2nd Low Altitude Air Defense Squadron, keeps a lookout for hostile aircraft. The Avenger has a two-man crew and can operate during the day or night.

M270 Multiple Launch Rocket System

With its origins back in the 19th century – Congreve's rockets – and more recently in the form of the World War II Katyusha, the MLRS is an artillery weapon system that supplements cannon artillery fires by delivering large volumes of firepower. It delivers freeflight basic and Extended Range (ER-MLRS) rockets and Army Tactical Missile System (ATACMS) Block I missiles. Growth programs are underway to extend the range and accuracy of the rockets and to upgrade the launcher to fire precision guided rockets and missiles to include Guided MLRS (GMLRS) and ATACMS/Brilliant Antiarmor Submunition (BAT)

Block II weapons

M109A6 Paladin Howitzer

The Paladin is the most technologically-advanced self-propelled cannon system in the US Army. The "A6" designation identifies several changes to the standard model—a fully automated FCS, a computer-controlled gun drive, improved ballistic and nuclear, biological and chemical protection and is capable of firing within 45 seconds from a complete stop. Its ammunition has 18.6 miles (30km) range with HE RAP and M203 propellant.

Patriot Antimissile Missile System

The Patriot is designed to provide defense against aircraft, cruise missiles, and tactical ballistic missiles. Each of eight launching stations contains four ready-to-fire missiles sealed in canisters that serve the dual purposes of shipping containers and launch tubes. Patriot's fast-reaction capability, high firepower, ability to track numerous targets simultaneously, and ability to operate in a severe electronic countermeasure environment are significant improvements over previous air defense systems. Currently underway is the Patriot Advanced Capability-3 (PAC-3) upgrade program that will incorporate significant upgrades to

BELOW: Soldiers from the 31st Air Defense Artillery Brigade load a Patriot missile onto a transfer vehicle at McGregor Test Range, NM, during Exercise "Roving Sands."

the RS and ECS, and will add the new PAC-3 missile, which utilizes hit-to-kill technology for greater lethality against TBMs armed with weapons of mass destruction. Additionally, it will be possible to have up to 16 PAC-3 missiles per launcher, increasing firepower and missile defense capabilities.

AH-64 Apache Longbow attack helicopter

The McDonnell Douglas AH-64 Apache helicopter is the US Army's main attack helicopter utilizing the Hellfire antitank missile, 2.75-in (70mm) rockets, and 1.2-in (30mm) chain gun. The AH-64D Apache Longbow has an upgrade of the Hellfire targeting system making it capable of full fire-and-forget all-weather, use. Longbow integrates a mast-mounted millimeter-wave fire control radar, a radar frequency interferometer, and a radar frequency fire-and-forget Hellfire II missile on the Apache. The modernized Apache heavy attack team will now be able to provide a truly coordinated rapid-fire capability (servicing 16 separate targets within a minute).

LEFT: A Hughes AH-64 Apache advanced attack helicopter firing 2.75-in (70mm) rockets at a ground target.

BELOW: The UH-60 Blackhawk, the US Army's battlefield utility helicopter, gained notoriety known after its use in Somalia and the film "Blackhawk Down".

UH-60 Blackhawk Helicopter

The Sikorsky Blackhawk provides air assault, general support, aeromedical evacuation, command and control, electronic warfare, and special operations uses. The UH-60 utility tactical transport helicopter has enhanced the overall mobility of the Army, due to improvements in troop capacity and cargo lift capability, compared to the UH-1 Huey it replaces. An entire 11-person, fully equipped infantry squad can be lifted in a single Blackhawk; it can reposition a 4.14-in (105mm) howitzer, its crew of six, and up to 30 rounds of ammunition in a single lift.

Tactical Unmanned Aerial Vehicle (TUAV)

A TUAV is designed to provide reconnaissance, surveillance, and target acquisition (RSTA) at an initial range of 31 miles (50km), day or night, in limited adverse weather conditions with a future, objective range extending to 124 miles (200km). A TUAV system consists of two ground control stations, a minimum of three air vehicles (AVs), modular mission payloads, and launch and recovery equipment. The

ABOVE: US Army Blackhawk helicopters lift off at Cairo West Air Base, Egypt, during Exercise Bright Star.

RIGHT: US Army UH-60L Blackhawk helicopters load soldiers at Allen Army Air Field.

BELOW: An Army National Guard soldier conducts maintenance on the tail rotor of a UH-60Q Blackhawk medevac helicopter in Romania.

complete TUAV system can be transported by two C-130 aircraft. Mission capability will be enhanced as advanced mission payloads become available, maximizing battlefield digitization to increase the effectiveness of other weapon systems.

CH-47 Chinook/Improved Cargo Helicopter

Designed by Boeing Vertol in the 1950s, the Chinook first flew in 1961. A medium transport, the army uses it for the transport of ground forces, supplies, and ammunition. The CH-47 is the Army's only heavy-lift cargo helicopter capable of cargo movement of payloads greater than 9,000lb (4,082kg). It is due for an upgrade—the CH-47F Improved Cargo Helicopter program will remanufacture 300 of the current fleet of 431 CH-47Ds, install a new digital cockpit, and make modifications to the airframe to reduce vibration. Other airframe modifications reduce the time by about 60 percent required for aircraft tear down and build-up after deployment on a C-5 or C-17.

RAH-66 Comanche Helicopter

The RAH-66 Comanche is a next-generation helicopter, designed to perform armed reconnaissance and light-attack reconnaissance missions. The Comanche will significantly expand the Army's capability to conduct reconnaissance operations in all battlefield environments, day or night, and during adverse weather. The Comanche will replace three types of helicopters (AH-1, OH-58, and OH-6) that currently perform the armed reconnaissance mission. Currently Comanche is in the last phase of development, with two prototype aircraft in active flight test status.

Kiowa Warrior

The Kiowa Warrior is a rapidly deployable, lightly armed reconnaissance helicopter. The Kiowa Warrior

BELOW: Two US Army CH-47 Chinook helicopters sling load Humvees at Allen Army Airfield, Fort Greeley, Alaska.

includes advanced visionics, navigation, communication, weapons, and cockpit integration systems. The mast-mounted sight (MMS) houses a thermal imaging system, low-light television, and a laser rangefinder/designator. These systems allow target acquisition and engagement at stand-off ranges and in adverse weather conditions. The Kiowa Warrior is rapidly deployable by air and can be fully operational within minutes of arrival. The armament systems combine to provide antiarmor, antipersonnel, and antiaircraft capabilities at standoff ranges. Although Kiowa Warrior fielding is complete, the Army is currently installing a series of safety and performance modifications to keep the aircraft safe and mission effective until it is retired.

Family of Medium Tactical Vehicles (FMTV)

The Family of Medium Tactical Vehicles (FMTV) consists of a common truck chassis that is used for several vehicle configurations in two payload classes and two tactical trailers with complementary payloads. The Light Medium Tactical Vehicle (LMTV) is available in van and cargo variants and has a 2.5-ton payload capacity. The Medium Tactical Vehicle (MTV) has a 5-ton payload capacity and consists of the following models: standard- and long-wheel base cargo (with and without matériel-handling equipment), tractor, wrecker, and dump truck. The FMTV is replacing the over-aged and maintenance-intensive trucks currently in the medium tactical vehicle fleet.

The Army has awarded a new four-year contract to Stewart & Stevenson Services and they have begun full production of the FMTV A1 series. The FMTV A1 includes a 1999 Environmental Protection Agency-certified engine, with an upgraded transmission, electronic data bus, an anti-lock brake system and interactive electronic technical

BELOW: The Family of Medium Tactical Vehicles will replace standard trucks in US Army use.

ABOVE: The Family of Medium Tactical Vehicles (FMTV) consists of a common truck chassis used for several vehicle configurations.

manuals. Also under contract are the new FMTV 2.5-ton and 5-ton tactical trailers that have the same cube and payload capacity as their prime mover.

The Future

Although the US Army infantryman still carries a weapon that is almost unchanged from the one his father carried in Vietnam, there are some major changes happening to the soldier's gear. The M16 is likely to remain the soldier's primary weapon for many years to come, but there are some very interesting new systems currently being fielded to make it and its user more efficient and effective.

Actually, the whole process of using advanced technology for the common foot soldier goes back almost as far as the M16, to the war in Vietnam. Back in the late 1960s the Army started introducing the first generation of night vision systems, particularly the early "starlight" scopes used on some weapons. At the time, there were lots of problems with this technology and lots of critics who said it would never work. Well, the scopes worked well enough to start picking off the VC and NVA in the middle of the night, and that changed the nature of battle in a significant way.

Night vision technology has been developed to such a high state of perfection that soldiers now depend on it and battle doctrine is written around its use. The same is true of GPS that lets a squad leader know exactly where he is, in the middle of the night, far behind the lines. These and other technologies have confounded the critics—they are dependable, durable, and give the American foot soldier another little edge when the poop hits the propeller.

There is currently another program developing another kind of technology. As with NVG and GPS, it is having its teething problems and it has its critics. This technology is based on digital communications and an integrated system of devices that combine different kinds of information from different places into one big, highly detailed, almost-real-time resource. At the soldier-level, it is a package called "Land Warrior." At the battalion and brigade command level, it is a related package called FBCB2" (see page 184).

Land Warrior

The Land Warrior system makes a soldier look like something out of a Robo-Cop movie. His helmet has a small monocular display linked to a compact computer stowed in his pack. The display can show the soldier a map of the area, complete with symbology for enemy and friendly units, target sensor display (day or night), and navigational information. A Global Positioning System transmitter/receiver provides constant real-time information about the soldier's location—to both the soldier and to his parent command.

There are five basic parts to the Land Warrior system: First is a modified M4 carbine with laser-aiming pointer and a sight that includes video capture, a digital compass, thermal sensor, and close-combat optics. If it all works as advertised, that will let a soldier shoot around corners, exposing only the weapon and his hands, while aiming the carbine with the video display.

Part of the kit includes a new helmet that is quite a bit lighter than the current kevlar but with improved ballistic protection. And, it reduces somewhat the problems some soldiers had with limited visibility and restricted hearing when using the standard-issue kevlar.

The whole package weighs 16lb, including body armor. That sounds like a hefty addition to the soldier's load but he actually will be lighter by a half-pound because the new body armor is so much lighter than the old.

The virtues of the system are in its ability to improve everybody's situational awareness—the soldier on the ground will have a better idea of where the bad guys are, and where the good guys are, too. The soldier's commanders will also know where the squads and fire-teams are, when they are moving and when they are taking a break.

The possibilities for mischief and mayhem with Land Warrior technology are endless. If a squad leader can transmit video from his weapon sight back to the TOC, there is always the possibility that it will be intercepted by the opposing team or (worse yet) by CNN.

And with the squad leader or platoon leader on an electronic leash, there will always be the temptation for those on high to micromanage tactical operations. Digital, real-time, secure communications will allow

ABOVE: Modern training aids do much to enhance tactical awareness in combat—much as the USAF's Top Gun programs achieved for air-crew.

squad leaders – under fire and in close contact with the enemy – to get messages that sound something like: "HATCHET ONE SIX, THIS IS GUNFIGHTER CONTROL; THE SECRETARY OF DEFENSE THINKS YOU SHOULD SHIFT YOUR POSITION ONE HUNDRED METERS TO THE WEST … DO YOU COPY?"

To which the squad leader is likely to do what his Vietnam era forebearers did … he'll reply "GUNFIGHTER CONTROL, HATCHET ONE SIX—DID NOT COPY YOUR LAST; TRANSMISSION WEAK AND BROKEN. HATCHET ONE SIX, OUT." Then he will turn off the radio and drive on with the mission.

FBCB2 and the Tactical Internet

One of the great developments in modern military technology, and another product of the whole Force XXI program, is a pair of linked developments nobody will want to shut down. One is called FBCB2, and that stands for *Force XXI Battle Command, Brigade and Below*. FBCB2 is primarily a software program that allows lots of players on the battlefield talk to each other in a controlled, focused way. Each of these players has a computer and GPS receiver/transmitter, all linked together by secure radios in what is called a Tactical Internet. The name is complicated but the basic idea behind it is simple—put everybody on the same sheet of music, all the time, from the squad leader and his fire-teams to the brigade commander in his TOC.

In essence, FBCB2 connects all the players in an operation on a wireless, secure, real-time internet. All the Bradleys, most of the HWWMVs, and all the combat leaders are equipped with a compact, rugged, computer. This computer is tied to a GPS system that provides continuous position updates and is linked to a very high resolution display, a keyboard, and a stylus. The display uses "touch screen" technology and standard menus similar to those found on any PC or Apple computer. But unlike your home computer, FBCB2 will show you exactly where you are, in near real-time, exactly where all the other "friendlies" are, where the enemy is reported to be, all superimposed on a very detailed map that scrolls and zooms as required.

If one of your scout Bradleys spots an enemy tank, they will laze it. That laze will provide both a precision bearing and a precision distance from an accurately known position, and the enemy tank can be automatically displayed on everybody's display. The combination of very accurate information with near real-time display and the ability to share this information with everybody who needs to know is going to revolutionize the conduct of some kinds of infantry operations.

The system allows the transmission of ACE (ammunition, casualty, equipment) and spot reports, orders, and communications of all kinds—complete with address books just like most of us use for office email. But unlike most office computers, the screen is touch sensitive—you work your way through menu items by pressing icons on the screen, as well as making keyboard entries.

Line-of-Sight Antitank (LOSAT) weapon system

LOSAT is designed to provide highly lethal, accurate missile fire, effective against heavy armor systems and field fortifications at ranges exceeding tank main gun range, reducing the light infantry force lethality shortfall against heavy armor. The Line-of-Sight Antitank (LOSAT) weapon system consists of four hypervelocity Kinetic-Energy Missiles (KEM), and a Second Generation Forward-Looking Infrared (FLIR)/TV acquisition sensor, mounted on an airmobile HMMWV chassis.

Objective Individual Combat Weapon (OICW)

The OICW will replace selected M16 rifles and M4 carbines. The modular, dual-barrel OICW will combine the lethality of 0.8-in (20mm) airbursting munitions, 0.22-in (5.56mm) NATO ammunition, with a full-solution fire control to affect decisively violent and suppressive target effects and to greatly improve small arms performance. This fire control will incorporate a laser rangefinder, ballistic computer, direct view optics, video sight, electronic compass, thermal capability, and a target tracker.

The OICW's high explosive air bursting munitions will be capable of defeating not only exposed targets, but those in defilade (targets that have taken cover behind structures, terrain features and/or vehicles), a capability lacking in current rifles and carbines. The OICW will provide an overmatch in

ABOVE: Laser training aids and other modern systems increase the realism – and therefore the usefulness – of modern training .

system effectiveness while increasing the versatility and survivability of the soldier by:

- doubling the infantryman's stand-off range to 1,094 yards (1,000m);
- providing effective day/night operation; and
- providing significant improvements in lethality and target effects.

XM777 Joint Lightweight 6.1-in (155mm) Howitzer (LW155)

The XM777 Joint Lightweight 6.1-in (155mm) Howitzer (LW155) is a joint Marine Corps/Army program, in which the Marine Corps funds the howitzer research, development, test, and evaluation (RDT&E) and the Army funds the RDT&E for Towed Artillery Digitization (TAD) and other automation enhancements. It will replace the M198 howitzer as a general support system for Army light forces. The Marine Corps will use it in direct support, replacing existing cannon systems. The XM777 incorporates innovative designs to achieve lighter weight, without sacrificing the range, stability, accuracy, or durability of the current system. The lighter weight is achieved through lower trunnion height and the use of high-strength titanium, a primary component of the lower carriage and cradle assembly.

Chow

If there is one great Army tradition, it is that soldiers bitch about their chow. If the mess hall recruited Sergeant Wolfgang Puck and Corporal Julia Child to prepare Châteaubriand, a proper Caesar salad, good French bread, excellent wine, with some Stilton cheese and 100-year-old port to follow, you can bet that ten soldiers out of a hundred will be complaining about the meal.

But you don't hear quite as much whining about the chow these days as back in the legendary "old"

ABOVE: Force morale is essential for efficient operations and the old maxim "an army marches on its stomach" is as true today as it was in the 19th century.

army. Millions of soldiers survived in the field on C-rations (or "C-rats" to an entire generation) and before that the dreary K-rations of our World War II forefathers. C-rats weren't too bad, if you like canned lima beans and ham, but almost nobody did. The little boxes often contained a chocolate bar that seemed to be manufactured from petrified chocolate—it wouldn't melt in the heat or in your mouth. The author of this section survived for much of a year in Vietnam on canned pound cake and fruit cocktail, for which he diligently searched through cases of rations, leaving lima beans for others less fortunate.

MREs

Despite what the troops call MREs – "Meal, Rejected by Ethiopians," or "Meal, Ready to Excrete" – the initials actually stand for Meal, Ready to Eat, and they are amazingly good. Instead of cans, the MRE uses pouches to keep the food fresh. There are about 12 entrées, including a couple of vegetarian options—chicken with rice, spaghetti and meat sauce, red beans and rice, beef stew, chili con carne, chicken stew, and others.

Each MRE is packed in a pouch that provides some protection against the inevitable rough handling for anything that goes to the field. The packet fits neatly in a BDU pant pocket or in the outside pockets of a backpack.

Inside the pouch is the entrée, a packet containing two large, thick, extremely dry crackers, a tube of peanut butter or jam, sometimes a pretty good little fudge bar, and a packet of either cocoa or kool-aid-type drink (called invariably "bug juice"). Current pouches contain a wonderful addition, a little chemical heater that is activated with a small amount of water—it will heat your entrée (and, if it is chilly, yourself) for about 15 minutes. There is also an accessory packet with an impossibly small quantity of toilet paper, a book of water-resistant matches (although the old five-pack of extremely stale cigarettes found in C-rats are gone), a little moist

ABOVE: A US Marine and a British Royal Marine chat while heating up English rolled oats as they break for chow.

towellette, some hard candy or gum, and—an inspired addition—a very tiny bottle of hot sauce. This latter component is big enough for just one serving for most soldiers, and adds horsepower and spice to anything.

Tray Rats

MREs are generally issued individually and used by soldiers when they are out in the weeds, away from the unit, but once every day in the field or so the platoon sergeant will try to get hot chow for the men. In the old days, that meant that the company cooks set up a field kitchen, did their best to fabricate soggy pancakes, scrambled eggs, and half-cooked bacon. The soldiers had mess kits to receive this issue, all of which was slopped together in a somewhat disgusting mélange. After the meal, the mess kit was cleaned in a garbage can filled with lukewarm water, soap, and the dregs of previous cleaning efforts. The result was that the mess kits didn't get very clean and the soldiers often got sick. But no more.

The company cooks still provide hot chow, and sometimes they prepare it from scratch (when it is officially called "A rations") in the field, but it is often trucked out in insulated marmite containers. But even more often they show up with Tray Rations, or "t-rats," and a big stack of paper plates.

T-rats can be quite good, and some people love them. Not everybody loves every entrée but most are extremely good—particularly, in the experience of the author, the canned omelet and the crumb cake. Others include sliced turkey, chicken, pork, hamburgers, sausage links, and the ancient and honorable SOS (as it has been called since World War II—"shit on a shingle," or creamed beef on toast).

These are flat aluminum "cans" about 14in by 20in. They can be heated in hot water, on top of a truck or tank engine, or even over a few bits of burning C-4. One tin will feed about 18 men, depending on their appetite and the generosity of the cooks. The problem with "T-rats" is that they start out warm and

RIGHT: Stacked boxes become tables as US Marines from the 26th Marine Expeditionary Unit eat at a field mess at Camp Monteith, near Cernica, Kosovo.

BELOW: Soldiers from the 5th Long Range Reconnaissance Patrol Company, Royal Thai Army, (right) share their traditional field chow with a member of the US Army's 6th Infantry Division (left).

BELOW, RIGHT: British Royal Marines (right) from 42 Commando offer hot water for making coffee and tea to US Marines from Kilo Company as they break for chow at Camp Lejeune, N.C.

the first half dozen men in line get hot chow. The next three or four get warm food, and the rest get theirs cold.

The US Army Reserve

The US Army Reserve is made up of ready-to-go combat support and combat service support forces that can move on short notice to give the active army the resources it needs to deploy overseas and to sustain combat troops during wartime, contingencies, or other operations. It is the Army's main source of transportation, medical, logistical, and other units, and it is the Army's only source of trained individual soldiers to augment headquarters staffs and fill vacancies in units.

The United States has always relied on a very small Regular Army augmented in time of crisis by militia or civilian volunteers. The training and preparedness of these troops was always suspect at best and non-existent at worst—something that cannot be tolerated today.

Today's US Army Reserve consists of more than a million men split into three categories—the Selected Reserve, the Individual Ready Reserve, and the Retired Reserve, totaling more than 1,000,000 reservists, upon whom the government can call when needed.

The invasion of Kuwait by Iraq in 1990 led to the largest call-up of Reserve Component personnel since the Korean War. More than 84,000 Army Reservists provided combat support and combat service support to the Total Force in Southwest Asia and site support elsewhere.

A key step in the continued development of the Army Reserve took place in 1991 with establishment of the US Army Reserve Command (USARC) in Atlanta. The USARC has responsibility for command and control of Troop Program Units nationwide and the 65th Army Reserve Command in Puerto Rico. The Chief, Army Reserve commands

LEFT: The US Army's small number of regular soldiers is supplemented when required by more than a million reservists.

the USARC, and also serves as Deputy Commanding General for Reserve Affairs, US Army Forces Command (FORSCOM).

In December 1995, the president authorized the call-up of Reserve Component forces as part of America's support to the NATO peacekeeping forces in the Bosnia-Herzegovina area. Within a short period of time the Army Reserve provided civil affairs, postal, medical, engineer, transportation, psychological operations and firefighting units, the first arriving in Bosnia in mid-January 1996. The initial manpower ceiling from the Reserve Component was 3,888, with soldiers activated for up to 270 days. In May 1996, the ceiling increased to 7,000 to allow overlap of deploying and redeploying units and individual soldiers. The majority of Army Reservists ordered to active duty served as backfill for active Army soldiers in Germany, but substantial numbers pulled duty in Bosnia and Hungary.

Today, the Army Reserve has almost 40 percent of the Army's combat support (CS) and combat service support (CSS) units. With over 92 percent of those units assigned a role under Army regional operational plans, the USAR is positioned to support almost any type of mission worldwide.

The Army Reserve is in the final stages of its strength drawdown and unit reorganization plan. The fiscal year 1998 programmed end strength of 208,000 will mean a reduction of 35 percent since 1989, when America began reducing its armed forces (the USAR will take the largest cut of any Reserve Component). Future unit activations and inactivations, tied to the off-site agreement with the Army National Guard, will reinforce the Army Reserve's core competency of combat service support.

The Army Reserve of the 21st century, with its core competency firmly planted in combat service support, will be a more relevant and better trained cornerstone of our nation's defense. While managed change is still in the Army Reserve's future, the basic values of its citizen-soldiers—duty and selfless service—will remain steadfast.

TOP RIGHT and RIGHT: Battlefield communication systems are likely to see major improvements as new technology comes in. FBCB2 and the Tactical Internet will be the first stage of this.

NAVAL WEAPONS

Since the end of World War II the US Navy has deployed a wide spectrum of weapon systems designed to enable its ships to fight and survive at sea. The main strike power was vested in the aircraft of the various Carrier Air Groups and considerable effort was put in to systems designed to defend task forces from all forms of aerial, surface, and undersea threats. In particular, given the size and power of the Russian submarine fleet, antisubmarine warfare (ASW) was given a very high priority. Amphibious warfare, involving landing forces against opposition, also needed support weapon systems, but these were generally limited to covering the immediate beachhead area.

In the last decade of the 20th century the end of the Cold War considerably lessened the likelihood of a major conflict between superpowers, but in its place US forces have been involved in an almost continuous series of small wars and peacekeeping actions including the Gulf War in 1991, subsequent strikes against Iraq in 1994, the various Balkan conflicts which followed the break up of the former Yugoslavia, and action in Afghanistan. The latter resulted from the September 11, 2001 terrorist attack against America and will almost certainly be followed by further action against states deemed to pose a threat to the US and other nations.

As these wars and actions have occurred, it has become apparent that the US Navy has had to reconsider its prime role and reevaluate the weapons needed to support this type of warfare. Instead of blue water oceanic deployments, US ships are now engaged in so called Littoral Warfare in which the target and objectives are land, rather than sea based. This poses a whole host of problem scenarios, which have to be faced and overcome.

In order to successfully engage land targets, ships must operate much closer to hostile shores where they can come under attack from land-based aircraft and missiles, and where ASW operations are much more complex in relatively shallow, littoral waters. From an offensive viewpoint, naval weapon systems must be capable of striking deep inland. Tactical cruise missiles now form a vital part of the US naval armory and even conventional guns have been

RIGHT: USS *McFaul*, an Arleigh Burke class AEGIS destroyer commissioned in 1998. This view clearly shows the phased arrays of SPY-1D radar set into the sides of the bridge superstructure. Also of note is the single SPG-62 target illuminating radar atop the bridge.

74

ABOVE: The nuclear-powered USS *Virginia* was one of a class of four built in the mid-1970s. Heavily armed for their time, they lacked AEGIS air defense systems and were retired in 1998.

BELOW: Built during World War II, the Iowa class battelships played an active part in the Gulf War. With limited modernization their land attack capability was improved by Tomahawk TLAM missiles.

RIGHT: USS *Spruance* (DD 693), lead ship of a class of 31 ships. On the foredeck is a Mk. 45 5-in (127mm) gun and immediately in front of the bridge are the silos of the 64 cell Mk. 41 Vertical Launch System (VLS). Atop the bridge is a single Mk. 15 Phalanx Close In Weapon System (CIWS).

BELOW: For self protection all US carriers are fitted with the Mk. 15 Phalanx and the RAM short range missile system. These can be seen either side of the forward flight deck in this view of the USS *Harry S Truman* (CVAN 75).

improved to offer accurate fire support far inland from coasts and beachheads.

In this section all major US naval weapon systems are described and it is noticeable how many are now focused to support the new appreciation of the Navy's role in the post-Cold War era.

Missiles—Strategic and Land Attack

Trident

The most powerful weapon in the US Navy's arsenal, and probably one of the most destructive weapon systems ever devised, is the Trident submarine launched ballistic missile (SLBM). In its most developed D5 form, this has a range of 6,500nm (12,000km) and can carry up to 12 Multiple Independent Reentry Vehicles (MIRV) each with a 100 or 475 kiloton (maximum) nuclear warhead. The destructive power embodied in a single Trident II999 missile can barely be imagined, and the awesome potential of a full 24 missile complement carried by one Ohio class nuclear powered strategic missile submarine (SSBN) does not bear contemplation.

The original Trident I became operational in 1977 aboard the USS *Francis Key Scott,* but the US Navy first deployed strategic missiles at sea in 1960 when the 1,200nm (2,222km) range Polaris A-1 was test fired from the newly commissioned USS *George Washington*. Further development led to the Polaris A-3 with a range of 2,500nm (4,630km) and this remained in service until 1977. In the meantime it had been supplanted by the Poseidon SLBM, which entered service in 1970, and offered an increase in

ABOVE: USS *Wisconsin,* last of the great battelships which once rule the seas with 16-on (406mm) guns in the Norfolk Naval shipyard.

LEFT: The US Navy amphibious assault ship USS *Wasp* comes to the aid of the merchant cargo vessel *Sea Land Mariner* in the Mediterranean.

RIGHT, ABOVE: The USS *Theodore Roosevelt* conducts a Vertical Replenishment weapons on-load with the ammunition ship USS *Santa Barbara* as they steam in the waters off the Virginia coast.

RIGHT, BELOW: The USS *Vincennes* steams in front of three other classes of USN ships as they operate in the Pacific Ocean.

range to a maximum of 3,200nm (5,926km), although the more significant improvement was in the payload which could consist of up to 14 warheads compared to a maximum of six carried by Polaris. Poseidon remained operational until 1991, when as result of international treaty agreements, it was decided to decommission the ten Benjamin Franklin class SSBNs which still carried this missile.

Successor to both Polaris and Poseidon was the Lockheed Martin Trident I (C-4) whose development could be traced back to a study of US strategic forces in 1966. A requirement for a range of 6,000 miles (9,600km) was identified but a missile capable of this would be too large to be accommodated in the launch tubes of the Lafayette and Franklin class SSBNs then in service or building. Consequently the Trident I had a range of only 4,350nm (8,056km), although this represented a considerable increase over the older missiles and gave the US strategic submarine fleet a substantial increase in flexibility. Trident I was a three stage missile powered by solid fuel rocket motors. Overall length was 34ft (10.4m) and it weighed 31.75 tons at launch. (Polaris and Poseidon were single and two stage missiles respectively). The first Trident test firing took place in January 1977 and it became operational in 1979. Twelve Lafayette/ Franklin class SSBNs were converted to carry Trident I between 1978 and 1982, but these were all decommissioned in the early 1990s as the later Ohio class entered service.

The Ohio class SSBN were designed to carry the longer ranged Trident II (D-5) which has an overall length of 46ft (14m) and weighs 57.15 tons at launch. In fact the first eight Ohio's were armed with the older Trident I but this version has now been almost entirely superseded as a modernization program has updated the boats to carry the Trident II. Unlike earlier SLBMs, the Trident is capable of pinpoint accuracy thanks to a precision stellar-inertial guidance system augmented by GPS for terminal guidance. Consequently it can be used to accurately deliver non-nuclear warheads although the development of various cruise missile systems makes this an expensive way of delivering conventional ordnance.

LEFT: A Trident missile D4 is launched from the USS *John C Calhoun* during 1980s test firing. The Lafayette class were not large enough to carry the Trident D5, and were decommissioned in1994.

ABOVE: The US Navy provisions its strategic missile submarines at coastal bases in the states of Washington, South Carolina, and Georgia. The Ohio class submarines are designed to carry the 44ft (1.5m) long, 83in (2.1m) diameter Trident II missile.

LEFT: A torpedo room aboard the nuclear-powered ballistic missile submarine Ohio (SSBX-726).

Tomahawk Sea Launched Cruise Missile

The 1991 Gulf War saw the first operational use of a powerful new naval weapon system—the Sea Launched Cruise Missile (SLCM). Fired from installations mounted on the battleships *Wisconsin* and *Missouri*, and later from submarines positioned in the Red Sea, Tomahawk SLCMs were among the very first ordnance to hit strategic targets within Iraq. Although this was Tomahawk's baptism of fire, the missile system had been under development since 1974 and was initially deployed by the USN in 1983. General Dynamics were awarded the original development contract under the designation BGM-109 and the first Tomahawk test firing took place in 1976.

Tomahawk was originally envisaged as a submarine launched weapon and this immediately fixed the maximum dimensions as it was to be fired from a capsule loaded in a standard 21-in (0.5-m) torpedo tube. As developed, this version is ejected from the tube by the hydraulic torpedo firing gear and the 7,040lb (3,200kg) thrust Atlantic Research rocket booster is fired by a lanyard when the capsule is approximately 30ft (10m) ahead of the submarine. At this point the missile leaves the launch capsule and, angled up at 50°, accelerates to over 50mph (80kmph) before breaking the surface at which point an external protective shroud is cast off and the aerodynamic surfaces are extended. The 598lb (272kg) thrust Williams F107 jet engine is spun up by means of a starter cartridge ready to take over as the expended booster is detached. Nosing over into level flight the missile begins cruising toward the target.

Following closely on initial development of the submarine launched version, a number of other variants were proposed which included the short ranged antiship BGM-109B and the closely related land attack BGM-109C. Both of these carried conventional warheads as opposed to the nuclear armed BGM-109A fired from submarines, while the later

LEFT: The USS *Ohio* (SSBN-726) was the lead ship of a class of 18 SSBM commissioned 1981–97. They were specifically designed to deploy the Trident D5 strategic missile.

RIGHT: A Tomahawk is fired from a Vertical Launch System aboard the US Navy trials ship USS *Norton Sound*.

RIGHT: A completed Tomahawk undergoing final factory checks. The two engineers help convey its size.

BELOW: Tomahawk TLAM in flight. Note the aerodynamic surfaces and the scoop intake for the jet engine just under the rear of the missile body.

BOTTOM: Several warships were equipped to fire Tomahawk TLAM from a deck-mounted, armored four round launcher. These included the four Iowa class battleships and Virginia class cruisers. These are now decommissioned and all current surface warships utilize the Mk. 41 VLS.

D variant was similar to the C except that it carried a specialized submunitions warhead.

Although the antiship variant used relatively conventional guidance methods (inertial platform and active radar terminal homing) the others used a completely new system which relied heavily on digital computer techniques. This was known as TERCOM which stands for Terrain Comparison and is a technique of comparing a real time radar derived picture of the ground below the missile's flight path with a series of digitally stored spot heights for various sections of the route. Information derived from comparison of the two sets of data is used to establish position and update the missile's inertial navigation system. For the nuclear tipped missiles, this system offered a highly satisfactory degree of accuracy, although it was dependant on the provision of adequate amounts of mapping data, usually derived from satellite surveys. The Tomahawk's computer is capable of storing over 20 TERCOM maps which enable complex routings to be achieved, avoiding and decoying enemy defenses. The whole system is designated TERCOM assisted inertial navigation system (TAINS).

After launch, the Tomahawk is guided initially by its inertial navigation platform which is programmed with the required route. Between each TERCOM check the missile steers to preprogrammed waypoints in straight lines at predetermined speeds and altitudes. This ensures not only that it will reach the target but also that the precise time of impact can be

ABOVE: USS *Los Angeles* was the first of 51 similar nuclear-powered attack submarines commissioned between 1976 and 1996.

BELOW: USS *John Young* is a modern, multimission warship whose primary mission areas are offensive strike warfare and undersea warfare. *John Young* uses gas turbine power.

arranged to suit a specific tactical objective (e.g. to coincide with a conventional airstrike). Once in the vicinity of the target, guidance passes to a system known as the digital scene-matching area correlator (DSMAC). This uses a nose mounted TV camera from which images are compared with digitally stored images of the target or surrounding area. By steering the missile to give optimum correlation, the DSMAC guidance can achieve accuracies of around 30ft (10m), which is absolutely amazing after a flight of up to 700 miles.

The BGM-109B antiship variant (now known as TASM) was the first to enter service, and was carried aboard Los Angeles and Sturgeon class SSNs from 1983 and aboard surface vessels from 1984. Currently Tomahawk arms versions of the Spruance class, while the current DDG-51 Burke class are equipped to fire Tomahawks from the Mk. 41 vertical launcher which can also fire Harpoon, Vertical ASROC and Standard missiles. In 1985, a new launch system for submarines, consisting of 12 vertical launch tubes between the pressure and outer hulls, was introduced aboard the USS *Pittsburgh* (SSN 720), although in most submarines the missile is launched from conventional torpedo tubes.

The Tomahawk variant which saw service in the Gulf War was the BGM-109C, also called the Tactical Land Attack Missile (TLAM-C). It entered service in 1986 and carries a 1,000lb (455kg) HE warhead. At the start of the war it was reported that the US Navy had some 900 TLAM-Cs in service, of which around 500 were deployed in the region. In the first two weeks of hostilities no less than 300 missiles were launched, including at least one on January 19, from a submarine, although the majority came from two battleships. Since the Gulf War, Tomahawks have been fired operationally in the September 1995 Bosnia strike (Deliberate Force), strikes against Iraq in 1996 (Desert Strike), and more recently against Al Qaida targets in Afghanistan. Many of these were fired from submarines, including British Trafalgar class SSNs which are now armed with Tomahawk following successful firing trials by an RN SSBN in 1998. Since 1994, the latest Block III TLAM-C, deployed by both the USN and RN, has a range increased to 914nm (1,693km) and has a GPS back-up to the TAINS.

The nuclear armed TLAM-N (originally BGM-109A) is now capable of ranges up to 1,400nm (2,593km) at a cruising speed of Mach.0.7 and can

carry a 200 kiloton nuclear warhead. The adaptability and relative low cost of this weapon, combined with the restrictions of the START treaty mean that no more Trident armed SSBNs are likely to be built and their successor is the new Virginia class SSNs due to enter service from 2004 onward. These will be armed with TLAM-N and TASM, as are the three Seawolf SSN and there are also plans to convert some Ohio class SSBN to carry up to 154 Tomahawk missiles in 22 vertical launch silos.

The Tomahawk missile has proved to be most effective weapon system and enables warships to strike accurately at precise targets hundreds of miles inland. Before the demonstration of its capabilities under wartime conditions, its true potential had not been understood by many strategists but the Sea Launched Cruise Missile is now established as one of the prime assets of American seapower. To date some 950 TLAMs have been fired in action with an 85 percent on-target success rate.

SLAM—Stand-off Land Attack Missile

The successful development of cruise missiles led in the 1980s to a Navy requirement for a shorter ranged missile employing similar technology for use by tactical aircraft such as the carrier based F-18 Hornet. In this case the object was to provide the aircraft with the means to launch precision strikes from a distance in excess of 50 miles (80km), outside the range of the target's air defense systems.

In an effort to reduce costs and lead times it was decided to base the new weapon, known as the Stand-off Land Attack Missile (SLAM), on the existing air launched McDonnell Douglas AGM-84 Harpoon antiship missile. Following the award of the development contract, trials began in 1987 and McDonnell Douglas delivered the first SLAM to the US Navy from its production facility at St Charles, Missouri, in November 1988.

Although SLAM used the airframe, warhead, propulsion, and control systems of the basic Harpoon, there were significant changes in the guidance system to reflect the change of role. For navigation a Global Positioning System (GPS) was incorporated to update the missile's inertial navigation system and allow a suitable flight profile to be followed. In the final stages of the attack an infrared seeker is activated and this sends a video image to the pilot or the bombardier/navigator, who then selects the specific aiming point by means of crosshairs on

LEFT: Artist's concept of the SSN-21 Seawolf class nuclear-powered attack submarine.

RIGHT: Sea SLAM is a ship launched version of the air launched SLAM. Principal difference is the addition of booster motor for initial acceleration at launch.

LEFT: A Stand-Off Land Attack Missile (SLAM) is launched from an F/A18. SLAM was first used operationally in the 1991 Gulf War against an Iraqi hydro-electric plant.

BELOW: A standard AGM-84 SLAM under the wing of a F/A18 Hornet. Note the hemispherical dome covering the IR seeker in the nose.

BOTTOM: SLAM-ER (Expanded Response) is currently in production for the USN. Designated AGM-84H, it offers increased range and upgraded guidance systems. External differences from the standard SLAM are the folding wings and revised nose geometry for the IR seeker

their cockpit display. Once the target is designated in this way, the seeker locks on to it and the missile completes the attack autonomously and with great accuracy. The use of an infrared seeker allows attacks to be carried out at night or in periods of poor visibility and, following a policy of using existing components wherever possible, this unit is identical to that used by the Maverick air-to-ground missile and the associated data link is taken from the Walleye guided bomb. The data link is extremely flexible, to the extent that the aircraft controlling the final attack may not be the one which launched the missile. This allows for considerable variation of tactics to further confuse defense systems and increase the chance of a successful attack.

Although still undergoing operational evaluation testing in 1991 when Operation "Desert Storm" commenced, the US Navy took the opportunity to try SLAM in action and it was successfully launched against an Iraqi hydro-electric plant. Since then the missile has passed into front line operational service and is currently available to all F/A-18 squadrons. SLAM has been the subject of improvements under a contract awarded to McDonnell Douglas in August 1994 for an Expanded Response program (SLAM ER). This retrofit program offers improved range and maneuverability through the use of redesigned wings, an improved and more lethal warhead, and new software to ease the task of the missile controller.

A ship launched version of SLAM, appropriately designated Sea SLAM, has been developed and this is entirely compatible with existing shipboard Harpoon command and launch infrastructure. There are some software modifications and a standard Harpoon missile booster kit is all that is required to convert the air launched SLAM into a Sea SLAM which can be fired from the standard Harpoon container launchers although some form of airborne control is still required for the final attack phase. Typically this could be carried out by the ship's helicopter. As well as the conventional high explosive warhead, Sea SLAM can also carry a variety of submunitions to attack soft targets or concentrations of armored vehicles. At present this version is not deployed by the US Navy.

BELOW: Harpoon antiship missile being launched from a fixed deck mounted canister. Note the rear mounted booster motor which will fall away on completion of the launch phase.

Antiship Missiles

RGM-84D/AGM-84/UGM-84 Harpoon

Harpoon is one of the most flexible naval weapon systems ever developed and is widely deployed throughout the navies of the United States and its allies. It was originally conceived as an air launched antiship weapon to be carried by P-3 Orion maritime patrol aircraft and the development program began around 1970 leading to the original AGM-84 Block 1 entering service in 1978. A requirement for long range led to the adoption of 600lb (1,320kg) thrust J402-CA-400 turbojet as the main propulsion and consequently the missile is subsonic with a cruising speed in the region of Mach 0.85. It is guided to

ABOVE: An RGM-84 Harpoon antiship missile speeds toward its target at Mach 0.85.

RIGHT: A Harpoon missile blasts off from a deck mounted canister. Most destroyers can be fitted with two quadruple canister launchers.

its target by an onboard inertial navigation system with an active, frequency agile, J-band radar being switched on at a predetermined point for the terminal homing phase. The initial Block 1A variant flew directly to the target but subsequent Block 1B and 1C versions were capable of complex maneuvers in order to evade defenses and countermeasures. In parallel with the air launched AGM-84, a ship launched RGM-84 was developed and this could be fired from fixed deck mounted canisters or from various launcher systems, now including the Mk. 41 VLS. This latter version differed from the AGM-84 in that it incorporated a solid fuel booster rocket for initial acceleration from the launcher. This subsequently fell away as the missile continued toward the target using its jet sustainer motor. The surface launched RGM-84 has a range of approximately 80nm, while the AGM-84 can manage up to 120nm (222km). A 488lb (227 kg) high explosive warhead is capable of causing significant damage to any surface vessel. The RGM-84 has an overall length (including booster)of 15ft (4.6m) and a body diameter of 1.13ft (0.343m). Wingspan over the fixed aerodynamic surfaces is 3ft (0.914m). Launch weight is 1,496lb (680kg). The air launched AGM-84 does not require a booster rocket and overall length is consequently shorter at 12.4ft (3.8m)

Britain's Royal Navy became a Harpoon customer in the wake of the Falklands War and their requirement for a sea-skimming capability resulted in the Block 1C variant which is the standard production version today. A Block 1D variant which featured a larger fuel tank and the ability to make a second attack if the first pass resulted in a miss was successfully tested in 1991, but production was shelved due to changing priorities with the end of the Cold War.

The US Navy's first operational use of Harpoon was in 1986 when AGM-84 missiles launched from A-6E Intruders sank two Libyan ships and further

ABOVE: This torpedo-shaped capsule is the container for a UGM-84 Sub Harpoon. The guide vanes at the rear ensure that the capsule reaches the surface at a suitable angle to discharge the missile.

LEFT: A standard quadruple container launcher for the Harpoon missile. Once installed aboard the ship, the missile requires no servicing and is permanently ready for activation and firing at short notice.

engagements against Iranian vessels in the Persian Gulf occurred in 1988. Harpoon was also used in the 1991 Gulf War.

Harpoon was also produced in the UGM-84 submarine launched version. The actual missile is enclosed in a torpedo sized capsule (ENCAP) which has positive buoyancy so that it floats to the surface after discharge from conventional torpedo tubes. Fins on the ENCAP ensure that it reaches the surface at a suitable angle for missile launch. At this point the capsule nose is blown off and the missile booster motor fired. One problem with the UGM-84 is that accurate long target information is not always available to the parent submarine and this may have to be provided by an external source such as an aircraft or surface ship. At shorter ranges, sonar derived information can provide accurate enough data for an attack. The UGM-84 arms all current US Navy attack submarines.

Harpoon was developed by the McDonnell Douglas company, now part of Boeing, and the missile family was originally envisaged to remain in service until 2015. However, constant improvements and upgrades have maintained Harpoon as a creditable weapons system and no replacement is currently scheduled. To date well over 6,000 missiles have been produced and it is in service with navies and air forces around the world.

AGM-119 Penguin

In US Navy service the Penguin antiship missile arms SH-60 Seahawk helicopters deployed aboard cruisers, destroyers, and the FFG-7 class frigates. Originally developed by Norway as a surface-to-surface missile to arm Fast Attack Craft, it proved to be most adaptable and can now be launched from ships, helicopters and aircraft.

ABOVE: The Norwegian designed Penguin antiship missile arms SH-60 and SH-2G Seasprite helicopters carried aboard destroyers and frigates. Note the folding fins which are deployed after launch.

BELOW: Artist's impression of a Penguin antiship missile being launched from a SH-60B helicopter whose search radar will have been used to provide target data prior to launch.

Its history goes back to the 1950s when the Norwegian Navy conducted a searching review of its role in the light of the massive growth of the Soviet Navy and a decision was made to concentrate on a force of small, fast, well-armed patrol boats and, in particular, the future importance of the surface-to-surface missile was recognized (even though no operational examples existed at the time). As a result, in 1962, development of a suitable missile was initiated under a contract awarded to Kongsberg, who at that time were heading up a European consortium that was about to commence production of the US designed air launched Bullpup missile for various NATO air forces. It was natural, therefore ,that several Bullpup components, including the warhead, should find their way into the new Penguin. The other significant feature was the guidance system, which relied on passive infrared for final target acquisition, as opposed to the more conventional radar seeker used by almost every subsequent antiship

TOP: An AGM-114B Hellfire missile roars off the rails of a US Navy SH-60 Seahawk helicopter toward a laser designated surface target during training off the coast of California.

ABOVE: An SH-60 Seahawk helicopter assigned to Helicopter Antisubmarine Squadron Seven hovers off the bow of the aircraft carrier USS *Enterprise*.

missile. This was partly for practical reasons, since at that time radar seekers were relatively bulky, but also because in the likely area of operations around Norway's rocky coast and steep sided fjords there would be considerable radar clutter to be overcome.

Although developed and produced in Norway, there was actually considerable US involvement in the program including financial assistance and the provision of test facilities. A total of 60 development and evaluation rounds were produced between 1964 and service entry in 1971, when it armed Storm class missile boats of the Royal Norwegian Navy. The original Mk. 1 Penguin weighed 750lbs (340kg) at launch and was powered by a Raufoss dual thrust solid fuel rocket motor. Housed in a fiberglass container bolted to the deck, the missile was launched by a two second firing of the boost stage after which the sustainer stage continued to accelerate the missile to its cruise speed of Mach 0.8 out to a maximum range of 12.4 miles (20km). Prior to launch the missile's inertial guidance system was provided with basic target data (e.g. bearing, range, rate of crossing, etc.) to enable it to close to within 3 miles (5km) at which point the infrared seeker was activated. During the cruise, the missile maintained a height of approximately 328ft (100m) using information derived from a pulsed laser altimeter (heady stuff for the early 1960s!). The 250lb (113kg) Mk. 19 Bulldog warhead was sufficient to cause significant damage, even to large ships. A missile could be activated and launched in two minutes, but this reaction time was cut to seconds if the seeker head cooling was already functioning. Time of flight was around 85 seconds to maximum range. A modified Mk. 2 with longer range was subsequently adopted and test firings of a Mk. 3 variant developed for launching from airborne platforms was test fired in 1984.

When the Norwegian Air Force developed the Mk. 3 for use aboard fast jets, the US Navy investigated the possibility of arming the standard SH-60B Seahawk helicopter with the missile in order to provide an effective antiship capability. The version selected for trials was designated Mk. 2 Mod. 7 and the first contract, for 64 missiles, was signed in 1989. In the meantime, a test program culminated in the first successful launch from an SH-60 in December 1989 and further firings in 1990. In US service the Penguin is designated AGM-119B and is in fact a hybrid, combining features of both the Mk. 2 and 3. Although air launched, the two stage motor of the Mk. 2 is incorporated to provide acceleration to cruise speed as the launch helicopter has a relatively low airspeed. However the guidance system is substantially the same as that of the Mk. 3 and incorporates a radar altimeter instead of the pulsed laser type used in the shipboard variants.

An obvious external difference between the two air launched versions is that the Mod. 7 has folding wing surfaces to facilitate storage aboard ship and carriage on the UH-60 weapon pylon. The use of the Raufoss two-stage, solid fuel, rocket motor reduces range to around 21 miles (34km) compared to 34 miles (55km) for the Mk. 3. Overall dimensions: length 9.8ft (3m), span 4.5ft (1.4m), 1.8ft/0.56m with wings folded and body diameter 0.9ft (0.28m).

The UH-60 is equipped with a Texas Instruments AN/APS-124 search radar which is used for target location and designation. Coordinates are fed to the missile's inertial guidance system and after launch, a preprogrammed route is flown to the point at which the IR seeker is activated. Alternatively, targets can be designated from visual sightings. For launch, the helicopter must have some forward airspeed to prevent an initial pitch up of the missile which free falls for less than half a second to allow the wings to extend before the booster motor phase ignites. Although the Mod. 7 does not have a sea-skimming capability, its small radar cross section, agility, and passive infrared homing system makes it difficult to detect and consequently gives it a good chance of defeating modern countermeasures including fast reaction CIWS.

AAW (Antiaircraft Warfare Missiles)

AEGIS/Standard

The Standard Missile is the US Navy's primary surface-to-air fleet defense weapon and its development goes back to the 1960s when it evolved as a replacement for the earlier Terrier and Tartar from which it utilized many components. The original SM-1 missile was produced in MR (medium range) and ER (extended range) versions, the former having an overall length of 14.4ft (4.4m) and was powered by a single-stage, dual thrust rocket motor, while the lat-

RIGHT: The Standard missile was developed from the Tartar and Terrier surface-to-air missiles, which armed destroyers, frigates and cruisers in the 1960s and 1970s. Photo shows a Tartar test firing aboard the trails ship *Norton Sound*.

BELOW RIGHT: An SM-1MR Standard missile on a single arm Mk. 13 launcher aboard a FFG-7 class frigate.

BOTTOM RIGHT: The Mk. 13 launcher is raised to the vertical position to allow missile loading from the magazine below.

ter featured two-stage booster and sustainer motors and consequently length was increased to 26ft (8m). Maximum ranges were approximately 25nm (40km) and 100nm (160km) respectively. The SM-1 employed a conventional command guidance system, with semi-active homing for the terminal phase, which required a target illuminating radar on the parent ship. SM-1R is now only deployed aboard Oliver Hazard Perry class frigates which utilize the SPG-60 fire control radar.

The larger Tioconderoga (CG-47) class cruisers and Arleigh Burke destroyers are armed with the developed SM-2MR/ER which is similar in to the SM-1 in terms of size and propulsion system but achieves greater flexibility and range through the introduction of a more sophisticated guidance system based on an onboard inertial platform—the first to be fitted to any tactical missile system. Terminal guidance is still by semi-active homing using an illuminating radar. Aboard the early CG-47 ships the SM-2MR was fired from a Mk. 26 twin launcher on the foredeck but later vessels incorporated the Mk. 41 VLS, as do all of the Arleigh Burke class destroyers which deploy the SM-2ER. The SM-2MR weighs 1,380lbs (621kg) at launch while the figure for the larger SM-2ER is 2,980lbs (1,341kg). Both attain speeds of Mach 2 and carry a high explosive fragmentation warhead triggered by a proximity fuze.

The current Standard SM-2 is an integral part of the AEGIS weapons system (named after the shield of Zeus in Greek mythology) based on the distinctive SPY-1 phased array radar which utilizes electronic scanning instead of the traditional rotating antenna associated with conventional radar. This enables simultaneous search and tracking functions, and allows AEGIS to meet its intended purpose of dealing simultaneously with multiple aerial targets. In the

face of such an attack, an AEGIS equipped ship can launch numerous Standard missiles in rapid succession and each is tracked toward its designated target by the SPY-1 radar. In the closing stages of the engagement, AEGIS directs an SPG-62 target illuminator briefly at the target while the SM-2 completes the interception using semi-active homing. The SPG-62 is then directed at the next priority target, which is already being closed by another SM-2. This method of engagement is significantly different from that used by the SM-1 and some non-AEGIS equipped ships deployed the SM-2, where the illuminating radar was required to track the target throughout the whole engagement, from missile launch to interception. In order to permit rapid multiple missile launches from the Mk. 41 VLS, a special version of the SM-2MR/ER, was produced in which the booster uses thrust vectoring instead of movable tail surfaces for directional control immediately after the launch.

Further development of the SM-2 was initiated to meet the Navy's requirement for a Theater Ballistic Missile Defense system (TBMD). The resulting Block IVA version was test fired in 1997 and successfully intercepted a ballistic missile target. However, the problems associated with producing a fully operational and effective TBMD capability have proved more difficult than anticipated and the program has currently been shelved.

ABOVE: A close up of the midships section of the USS *Winston S Churchill* (DDG-81) showing two more SPG-62 radars aft of the funnels.

RIM-7 Sea Sparrow

By the early 1960s, the US Navy began to realize that a considerable gap was opening up between the performance of a long-range system, such as Talos and Terrier, and the outdated short-range gun systems then in service. In order to save on costs and development time, the US Navy decided to adapt the highly successful AIM-7 Sparrow air-to-air missile for shipboard use as part of what was termed the Basic Point Defense Missile System (BPDMS).

ABOVE: USS *Arleigh Burke* (DDG51) was launched in 1989 as the lead ship of a class of AEGIS destroyer and is named after an able and distinguished destroyer captain (later admiral) who fought several successful actions in the Pacific during World War II.

LEFT: This schematic of the AEGIS weapon system gives some idea of the major components which together form a complex, but effective defense against multiple simultaneous air attacks. Core of the system is the SPY-1 phased array radar together with the SM-2 standard surface-to-air missile.

ABOVE: A standard eight-cell Mk. 29 launcher system for the Sea Sparrow. short range surface-to-air missile. This type of launcher arms the Spruance class destroyers and also a number of NATo warships.

BELOW: A Sea Sparrow missile leaps from the aft Mk. 29 launcher aboard a Spruance class destroyer. Maximum engagement range is in the order of 8 miles (12.8km), covered in less than 15 seconds at Mach 2.5.

The Sparrow missile itself was an early generation air-to-air missile, which had begun development in 1946 and eventually entered full-scale service in 1956. It has subsequently been updated several times and is still in widespread service today. The initial version selected for shipboard use was the AIM-7E which utilized semi-active radar homing whereby the missile homes onto reflected radar signals from a target illumination radar mounted on the launch vehicle (aircraft or ship).

BPDMS was a relatively crude system and suffered from a number of limitations, particularly against low flying targets. However, its relative simplicity and low cost led to its adoption by NATO as the basis for a standard short range antiaircraft missile system under the designation NATO Sea Sparrow Missile System (NSSMS). Development of this improved version followed from a Memorandum of Understanding signed by the US, Belgium, Denmark, Italy, and Norway in 1968 (subsequently The Netherlands and Germany joined the program) and Raytheon, the manufacturers, were awarded an initial contract for three systems. The first of these was fitted to the Knox class frigate USS *Downes*, which began test firings in 1972. NATO Sea Sparrow

differed from BPDMS in several key areas. The missile itself was the RIM-7H, which featured folding fins to fit a much smaller, purpose designed, lightweight, eight-cell launcher (Mk. 29). New digital electronics and components for the FCS were developed by companies from Italy, Denmark, and Norway while a new power driven Mk. 91 director incorporated an I/J band continuous wave radar for target tracking and illumination and also a TV camera for visual monitoring of the engagement. A complete NSSMS shipboard outfit weighed 28,648lbs 12.994kg), including the eight missiles in the launcher. Following successful trials, full production of NATO Sea Sparrow began in 1975.

Meanwhile in the United States development of the basic Sparrow missile continued and in 1980 tests began on a new version, the AIM-7M, which featured a monopulse radar seeker in the nose together with an on-board autopilot and other electronic improvements. These changes meant that target illumination was not required continuously, but only for mid-course corrections and terminal guidance. This, in turn meant that the launch vehicle could fire several missiles at different targets in rapid sequence. The new Sea Sparrow variant was designated RIM-7M and was capable of being fired by all existing systems. However, following successful tests,

ABOVE: A sequence of photos showing a VLS Sea Sparrow arching over onto the target bearing immediately after launch.

BELOW: The Mk. 91 fire control radar associated with the Sea Sparrow Missile System. There are separate transmit and receive aerials and this example also incorporates a boresighted electro-optical tracker between the antenna.

which began in 1981, a new vertical launch system became available for Sea Sparrow and the RIM-7M could be adapted for this mode of firing. Sea Sparrow missiles modified for VLS incorporate a jettisonable jet vane control unit (JVC). Bolted to the missile's tail section, the JVC has its own built-in processor and a hydraulic system that moves vanes within the rocket motor's exhaust to turn the missile on course to the target after the launch. As with all VL systems, this arrangement does away with complex launchers and offers a 360° coverage from a single installation.

Sea Sparrow is today in service aboard over 100 ships operated by ten navies and continued improvement has resulted in the current production version, the RIM-7P. The naval version of this multipurpose missile features folding wings and clipped fins to allow compatibility with all launch systems and can be fitted with a JVC for vertical launch. A new missile borne digital computer includes Erasable Programmable ROM chips, which allow quick and easy reprogramming of the guidance software to counter new threats. It also has an improved Low Altitude Guidance Mode, which enhances the discrimination of very low targets against a background that is heavily cluttered.

Other electronic improvements include a data link for mid-course guidance and built-in test circuitry to enhance maintainability and confirm readiness on the launcher. A further version is the RIM-7R, which incorporates an infrared guidance and homing system to complement the standard semi-active radar seeker. In addition, it has a more powerful rocket motor with a new autopilot to allow rapid response and high energy maneuvers against the late detection of high speed agile threats. The RIM-7R is compatible with existing launcher systems including the NATO standard Mk. 29 and the Mk. 41 and Mk. 48 VL systems.

BELOW: All US Navy carriers are armed with NATO Sea Sparrow for point defense, each ship carrying three Mk. 29 launchers. This example is being fired from the USS *John F Kennedy* (CV67).

ABOVE: A RIM-7 Sea Sparrow missile launches from the destroyer USS *Cushing* (DD985), a Spruance class destroyer completed in 1979. these ships carry a single Mk. 29 launcher abaft of the helicopter flight deck.

RIM-162 Evolved Sea Sparrow Missile (ESSM)

As its name implies, this is a development of the RIM-7P Sea Sparrow. A larger diameter after body contains a new rocket motor incorporating thrust vectoring for directional control and eliminating the need for winged control surfaces. The onboard guidance system is improved and a variety of operating modes are available. The ESSM has been designed to be fired from the standard Mk. 41 VLS with a quad pack of four missiles in each silo. It is also compatible with the Mk. 48 VLS and Mk. 29 multicell trainable launchers. An initial production order was placed in late 2001.

RIM-116 RAM (Rolling Airframe Missile)

The initial impetus for a new short range air defense system came from the German Navy in the mid 1970s, backed by a similar requirement from the Danish Navy, while the US Navy saw the new system as a candidate to arm the Tarawa class LHAs and the Iwo Jima class LPHs. Accordingly a joint US, German, and Danish program was launched and development began in 1976. Although loosely based on the Sidewinder, the new missile adopted a new and entirely novel method of aerodynamic control which was intended to increase maneuverability and safe weight by reducing the number of active control surfaces. In flight, the missile would slowly but continuously rotate under the effect of the four fixed tail fins, while directional control would be exerted by two canard surfaces on the forebody, these being sequentially deflected to provide the required change of course. A conventional missile, such as the original Sidewinder, would normally have required four canard control surfaces, each with its own actuator, so there was an immediate weight advantage to be gained by adopting the more unusual approach. This unique control system led to the name Rolling Airframe Missile (RAM), which was applied to the new weapon that was otherwise designated as the RIM-116A.

The final configuration meant that the only Sidewinder components incorporated in the RAM were the rocket motor, warhead, and fuze. The original infrared seeker was replaced by a more compact

ABOVE: A Marine AV-8A Harrier light attack jet aircraft lifts off the flight deck of the 820ft (250m) multipurpose amphibious assault ship USS *Tarawa*.

IR unit from the shoulder launched Stinger missile, but an additional target seeker in the form of RF (Radio/radar frequency) seeker was also incorporated. It was intended that the IR unit would home onto the forward aspect glint of a missile or aircraft or, alternatively, the RF seeker would home onto any radar emissions from the target (typically a radar-guided antishipping missile). A bonus of the rolling airframe concept was that only two RF aerials were required to obtain a three-dimensional tracking capability rather than the four needed in a conventional missile.

In action the missile would be fired in response to active radar, passive electronic, or optical warning and would be launched on a selected bearing and elevation. RF mid-course guidance is available, but RAM normally shifts to IR guidance for the final homing, although RF guidance can continue if weather conditions are unsuitable for IR functioning. This method of operation means that RAM is effectively a "fire and forget" system, a characteristic, which coupled with the relatively small size of the shipboard installation, opens up the possibility of providing small ships with the capability of dealing effectively with multiple targets. It is this capability which sets RAM apart from other similar short range defense systems.

It was hoped that the use of proven components in the missile and launcher systems would reduce the development period of the missile system, but in fact the reverse was true and when RAM finally entered service in the mid 1990s, it was some 12 years behind schedule. Most of the delays were due to practical problems related to the unique control and guidance system, but political and cost difficulties also contributed to the ever lengthening timescale.

The main US Contractor is the Hughes Corporation, and missile production is centered in Germany where it is carried out by the RAM System GmbH Consortium consisting of MBB, AEG-Telefunken and RTG. In US service the Mk. 31 RAM Guided Missile Weapons System (GWMS)

ABOVE: The Tarawa class amphibious assault ships were among the first to be armed with RAM for close-in self defense. Two Mk. 49 launchers are carried; above the bridge and starboard side, right aft.

includes a Mk. 49 Guided Weapon Launching System and a Mk. 44 Guided Missile Round Pack. The weapon system is extensively fitted throughout the amphibious warfare fleet including Tarawa class LHAs and Wasp class LHDs. Following various test firings and operational evaluations (OPEVAL), the first fleet firing of RAM was carried out from USS *Peleliu* (LHA-5) in October 1995.

Weighing 33lb (15kg), Ram carries a 6.6lb (3kg) proximity fused fragmentation warhead out to a range of 6 miles (10km) at speeds up to Mach 2. The initial production RIM-116A (Block 0) used a combination of RF/IR homing but the current RIM-116B (Block 1) missile has upgraded IR seeker which allows engagement of non-RF-radiating targets. Block 1 development trials were successfully completed in 1999; RAM was demonstrated against a variety of antiship missiles such as Harpoon and Exocet. Further software changes will enable other targets, such as helicopters, fixed wing aircraft, and small surface craft, to be engaged. RAM is also being tested in a new hybrid system known as SEA RAM which is described in the gun section of this chapter.

USW (Undersea Warfare) Weapons

RUR-5 ASROC

ASROC (the acronym for Antisubmarine Rocket) development began in 1955 to meet a USN requirement for an automated weapon system capable of deploying a Mk. 44 homing torpedo at ranges initially in excess of 10,000 yards (9,144m), which coincided with the ranges then being attained by contemporary shipboard sonars. The actual missile, designated RUR-5A, was simple enough and comprised an NPP (Naval Propellant Plant) boost solid fuel rocket with a thrust of 11,000lbs (4,990kg) in tandem with the Mk. 44 torpedo. Cruciform aerodynamic surfaces were attached to the rocket motor body and a parachute assembly was employed to lower the payload into the water after the booster separated on command from the fire control system.

LEFT: An eight-cell Mk. 112 ASROC launcher was standard when the anti submarine missile was introduced in 1960. It has now been almost entirely superseded by the Mk. 41 VLS although a few CG-47 class cruisers still retain the Mk. 26 twin Launcher.

RIGHT: An ASROC (RUR-5A) antisubmarine missile is launched from USS *Brooke* during fire power demonstrations.

BELOW, RIGHT: A huge underwater explosion following the launch of an ASROC antisubmarine missile during exercises from the destroyer USS *Agerholm*.

The missile had an overall length of 15ft (4m) (including the torpedo 8.75ft/2.67m long), body diameter of 12.75in (0.33m) and a wingspan of 2.8ft (0.85m). Launch weight was 957lbs (435kg).

In order to make effective use of the missile, a new sophisticated fire control system known as the MK. 114 Underwater Battery Fire Control System (UBFCS) was developed by the Singer Company under contract from Honeywell who were awarded the prime weapon system contact in 1956. In a typical engagement the target submarine is located by sonar and range and bearing data are passed to the Mk. 114 FCS, which then continuously computes the projected future target position while, at the same time, setting the separation point for the booster motor and launcher onto the correct bearing for firing. As soon as a solution is reached, the firing circuit is activated and the missile is launched. After separation the torpedo drops into the water close to the target, the parachute is released, it homes onto the submarine. ASROC was also designed to carry a W-44 nuclear depth charge instead of a torpedo and the accuracy of the system was enough to ensure target destruction in this mode of attack.

Although ASROC was designed to use a variety of launchers, the most common was the distinctive Mk. 112 eight-cell box which could rotate through 360°, while each vertical pair of boxes could be elevated to 45° for firing. Later ships could fire ASROC from the simplified Mk. 26 twin arm launchers, which could also fire Standard MR surface-to-air missiles. In this configuration each launcher is fed from one of three rotary drum magazines below decks, which respectively hold torpedo armed ASROC, depth charge ASROC or Standard MR SAMs, and loading of the appropriate weapon is controlled from the ship's operations room.

ASROC entered service with the US Navy in 1961 and the system was upgraded in 1965 when it was adapted to carry the Otto fuelled Mk. 46 lightweight torpedo (cf). The eight-cell Mk. 112 launcher became a familiar fitting on almost all new major US warships, although the first installations were aboard modernized wartime Gearing class destroyers which were converted to specialized ASW vessels under the FRAM 1 program begun in 1959.

When the Terrier SAM missile evolved into the current Standard surface-to-air missile, the dual purpose Mk. 26 launcher capable of handling ASROC was introduced and subsequently fitted to many ships completed from around 1976 onward. This included: the four Virginia class CGN, the Ticonderoga class AEGIS cruisers, and Kidd class DDGs. An exception to this were the 31 Spruance class DDGs, which continued to use the eight box launcher, although a new loading system was incorporated whereby the missiles where stowed vertically below the launcher that was in turn elevated to the vertical for reloading.

ASROC is widely deployed as the standard medium range ASW system in the US Navy and consequently it is unsurprising that the system has been widely adopted by foreign navies. Customers include Brazil, Canada, Greece, Italy, Japan, Pakistan, South Korea, Spain, Taiwan, Turkey, and Germany.

RIGHT: A Vertical Launch ASROC (VLA) emerges dramatically from its silo in a Mk. 41 launcher system.

RUM-139 Vertical Launch ASROC (VLA)

ASROC has proved adaptable to a wide range of launcher systems and the Arleigh Burke class DDGs introduced a new vertical launch variant of ASROC fired from the ship's Mk. 41 VLS launchers. This incorporates a total of 90 silos, which can carry either ASROC or Standard MR missiles. VLS ASROC (VLA), which entered service in 1987, has an increased range (9nm/16.7km) and is slightly longer than the standard version as it incorporates an additional booster for the launch and initial turn over maneuver. It carries a Mk. 46 Mod. 5 homing torpedo. The VLS system has also been fitted to later units of the Ticonderoga class AEGIS cruisers.

Prior to launch, the missile can be programmed through the Mk. 116 Underwater Fire Control System (UFCS) with tactical data from a wide variety of sources including hull mounted AN/SQS-53B sonar, NTDS data links with other ships and aircraft, AN/SQR-19 towed array sonar, and helicopter laid sonobuoys. The missile is housed in a canister, which is inserted directly into the launcher silo and no shipboard maintenance is then required prior to firing.

At one stage ASROC/VLA was scheduled to be replaced by the XMGM-52B Sea Lance intended to carry a Mk. 50 Advanced Light Weight Torpedo or an optional nuclear warhead. However, this was cancelled and VLA remains in service. A submarine launched version of ASROC (Subroc) carrying a W55 nuclear warhead was also deployed from 1962 onward, but this was withdrawn in the early 1990s.

Mk. 46 ASW Torpedo

The Mk. 46 is the standard NATO antisubmarine weapon and is deployed by a wide variety of ships, helicopters, and fixed wing aircraft. It became operational in 1967 and subsequently replaced the earlier Mk. 44 torpedo. Capable of speeds in excess of 45 knots and carrying a 98lb (44kg) PBXN-103 high explosive warhead, it has a maximum range of 12,000 yards (11km) although a more typical running distance is 8000 yards. The current version is the Mk. 46 Mod. 5 Neartip which has a length of 8.5ft (2.6m) and a diameter of 12.75in (0.33m). Its

ABOVE: An air drop version of the Mk. 46 torpedo shown on its handling trolley.

RIGHT: The Mk. 46 is designed to seek out and destroy high-speed submarines. These extremely effective weapons can be launched by more than 20 different launch platforms from antisubmarine warfare surface ships as well as aircraft.

total weight is 517lb (235kg) and propulsion is supplied by an Otto fuelled (monopropellent) two-speed reciprocating engine. With a running time of 6–8 minutes, the Mk. 46 commences a circular search on reaching the target area and uses Active or Active/ Passive homing in during the terminal phase. Aboard surface ships, the Mk. 46 is fired from the NATO standard deck mounted Mk. 32 triple torpedo tubes.

The Mk. 46 also forms an integral part of other weapon systems, notably the ASROC long-range ASW system described above. All current ASROC systems carry the Mod. 5 Neartip versions as the payload. The Mk. 46 Mod. 4 is a version specifically produced for incorporation in the CAPTOR mine system described later.

Mk. 48 Torpedo

The modern torpedo is a complex weapon system of possibly greater sophistication than airborne guided missiles and their design and development consequently spans decades rather than years. The Mk. 48 is no exception and initial work began in 1960, although it did not become operational with the US Navy until 1972. In its original form it could reach speeds of 55 knots and, at a slower speed of 40 knots, was capable of ranges up to 24nm (45km).

3 D TRACK

Propulsion was by means of a 500hp Otto cycle swashplate motor and total weight was 3,434lb (1545kg). The engine drives twin contra rotating propellers enclosed in a ducted shroud. Overall length was 19ft (5.8m) and the Mk. 48 was designed to be discharged from standard 21in (0.5m) torpedo tubes aboard surface vessels and submarines, although today there are no surface ships equipped in this way.

After firing, the Mk. 48 can follow programmed target search, acquisition, and attack procedures using active and/or passive homing for the final stages. Alternatively it can be wire-guided from the parent submarine throughout part or all of the engagement. If it misses the target at the first pass, it can then conduct multiple attacks until successful.

In 1978, development of a new heavyweight torpedo began, although this utilized many components of the basic Mk. 48. The resulting Mk. 48 ADCAP (Advanced Capability) became operational in 1988 and has now completely replaced the earlier version aboard all US submarines. The main difference related to the guidance and control system, which utilized modern digital technology, and the warhead fusing system was also upgraded. Engine performance was enhanced and additional fuel carried to allow an increase in range. The torpedo body shell was strengthened to allow greater diving depths, reputedly down to 3,000ft (900m), in order to counter deep diving Russian submarines such as the Alpha class. A speed in excess of 60knots has been quoted for the Mk. 48 ADCAP and range at 40knots is believed to be almost 30nm (55km). Both versions carry a 650lb (293kg) high explosive warhead but the ADCAP improvements resulted in an overall weight increase to 3,695lb (1,663kg).

Development of the Mk. 48 ADCAP continues with the emphasis on improved performance in shallow littoral waters against conventional diesel powered submarines and also to reduce its vulnerability to countermeasures.

ABOVE, LEFT: A Mk. 48 torpedo undergoes fuel tank stress measurement tests at the Naval Torpedo Station, Keyport, Washington.

LEFT: At 1.5 tons the Mk. 48 torpedo needs careful handling, as shown by this example being loaded aboard the USS *Pargo* a Sturgeon class SSN, at Cape Kennedy, Florida.

Mk. 50 Torpedo

Otherwise known as the Advanced Lightweight Torpedo (ALWT), the Mk. 50 is intended as the successor to the ubiquitous Mk 46. Development began in 1974 and OPEVAL started in 1990, although the latter highlighted some serious shortcomings, mainly software related and redesign and testing continued throughout the 1990s. Many problems were identified as being related to operator competency and familiarization and efforts have been made to improve matters in this respect, although at a cost of $70,000 for each exercise firing, training has been restricted. The current Mk. 50 Block 1 Upgrade torpedo can be air dropped from P-3 maritime patrol aircraft and a variety of helicopters including SH-2, SH-3, and SH-60. The Mk. 50 is also deployed in limited numbers aboard surface ships that also still carry substantial numbers of the earlier Mk. 46. Both can be fired from the standard Mk. 32 triple tubes.

The Mk. 50 torpedo is 111in (0.29m) long, has a diameter of 12.75in (0.3m), and weighs 775lbs (352kg). An active/passive sonar is mounted in the nose and torpedo operation is software controlled to define search and attack profiles. The warhead consists of a 100lb (45kg) shaped charge. Basically a fire and forget weapon, the Mk. 50 is faster (45kts) and deeper diving (to 2,000ft/600m) than the Mk. 46. Propulsion is by means of a closed cycle chemical reaction system utilizing a lithium-based fuel.

Mines

The US Navy no longer deploys specialist minelaying surface ships and all current mines in the US inventory are capable of being laid by aircraft or submarines. Today mines are a very sophisticated weapons systems and bear little resemblance to the traditional World War II contact mine. The most common air dropped mine is the Mk. 55, which contains a 1,275lb (577kg) HBX-1 high explosive charge and is produced in a variety of versions including Mod. 2 (magnetic influence), Mod. 3 (pressure/magnetic influence), Mod. 5 (acoustic/ magnetic influence), Mod. 6 (pressure/acoustic/magnetic), and Mod. 7 (dual channel magnetic).

This combination of influences, which can be set to detonate the mine and enable minefields to be set up, will only be activated by very specific targets. Total drop weight is in the region of 2,200lb (997kg).

The other common air dropped weapon is the Mk. 56, which is of similar size and weight, but is a moored magnetic influence mine.

Submarines are equipped to lay the Mk. 60 CAPTOR mine, which is a moored capsule containing a sensing element to detect and track targets, and a standard Mk. 46 homing torpedo. Intended primarily as an antisubmarine weapon, the Mk. 60 is capable of being moored in depths up to 1,000ft (300m), and its acoustic processor can track and classify targets. On acquiring a suitable target, the Mk. 46 is released vertically and then completes a standard engagement. The submarine version can be launched from standard 21-in (0.5-m) torpedo tubes and weighs just over 2,000lbs (907kg). There is also an air dropped version which is slightly heavier.

Submarines also carry the Mk. 67 SLMM (Submarine Launched Mobile Mine). This is basically an obsolete Mk. 37, conventional 21-in (0.5-m) torpedo modified to act as a mine. It is fired from the submarine and, at the end of its run, settles in a precalculated position enabling the submarine to remain clear of the area to be mined. The 326lb (148kg) HE warhead can be detonated by either pressure, magnetic, or acoustic target detection devices (TDD). The new Virginia class SSNs, due to be commissioned from 2004 onward, will be equipped with a mobile mine version of the Mk 48 torpedo.

The US Navy can also call upon large quantities of aircraft dropped Quickstrike mines. These are in effect standard Mk. 82/83/84 streamlined bombs, which are modified by the attachment of an exploder triggered by a TDD to act as a bottom mine in relatively shallow waters. These can be quickly produced and laid, obviating the need to hold stocks of more conventional moored mines.

Guns

The gun is the traditional naval weapon, although it has been eclipsed by the guided missile since World War II. However, it is making something of a comeback as modern technology is applied to the weapon itself, advance ammunition, and fire control systems. Although the US Navy has long since standardized on the 5-in (127-mm) gun, the recent emphasis on littoral warfare has led to the requirement for heavier weaponry, and the new DD(X) class destroyers will almost certainly carry a 6in (155mm) Advanced Gun System. This will fire a guided munition weighing approximately 120lb (54kg), substantially heavier than the 70lb (32kg) shell fired by the current Mk .45 5in (127mm)/54cal. although maximum range will be similar to that achieved by the later 5in (127mm)/62cal. Rate of fire will be about 12rpm.

The development of guided munitions, equipped with folding aerodynamic surfaces and boosted by rocket motors, opens the possibility of an entirely new type of gun with a fixed vertical barrel mounted within the ship. After firing, the projectile can be turned onto the desired trajectory by its guidance system in a manner similar to vertically launched missiles. Such a weapon would do away with complex turrets and mountings, and ammunition supply could be much simplified, leading in turn to increased rates of fire.

Technology of this nature is beginning to blur the distinction between guns and missiles. In the meantime, most ships carry relatively conventional gun systems, which are described next.

RIGHT: An impression of the 6.1-in (155mm) Advanced Gun System (AGS) aboard the DD21/DD(X) project.

Mk. 45 5-in (127-mm) Gun

The United States Navy has used the 5-in (127mm) gun as its standard medium caliber gun since it was introduced in 1907 as the secondary armament of contemporary battleships.

In World War II the ubiquitous dual purpose 5in (127mm)/38cal. weapon was used to arm everything from destroyer escorts up to battleships and aircraft carriers and, as a legacy, it has been widely adopted by many of the world's navies. In the postwar era, the USN developed automatic mountings that used the longer barreled 5in (127mm)/54cal. gun introduced at the end of the war. The first of these to see service was the Mk. 42 system, now replaced by the current lightweight Mk. 45 mounting.

The Mk. 45 gun system consists of two component groups, an upper and a lower structure. The former is defined as everything above deck level and includes all components necessary to load the ammunition, aim the gun, fire the ammunition, and eject the empty cartridge cases. To save weight, the gun and mounting is protected by a reinforced aluminum enclosure. The lower structure, below deck, is designed to deliver an uninterrupted ammunition supply to the gun and includes the gun system controls, loader drum, fuze setter, and the lower accumulator system to provide hydraulic power. An

ABOVE: A Mk. 45 5-in(127mm)/54 caliber gun aboard a US destroyer. The gun is enclosed in a lightweight gunhouse which is unmanned when firing.

BELOW: To provide greater support for amphibious operations, the Mk.45 5-in(127mm)/62 caliber gun is now entering service. The longer barrel and rocket assisted munitions give ranges in excess of 63nm (117km). Note the faceted "stealth" shape of the gunhouse.

RIGHT: A dramatic view of a Mk. 45 5-in(127mm)/54 caliber at the moment of firing. The 70lb (32kg) shell can be clearly seen in flight.

optional Mk. 6 lower ammunition hoist provides an ammunition load station and transfer mechanism for ships, such as cruisers and assault ships, whose magazines are located below the loader drum deck level. The whole system (excluding the optional hoist) weighs in at 49,000lb (22,226kg) which compares very favorably with the 149,930lb (68,150kg) of the previous Mk. 42 and is why the Mk. 45 is referred to as a "lightweight" system. The normal gun crew, none of whom are actually in the gunhouse, consist of six operators—a mount captain, a control panel operator, and four ammunition handlers. When action requirements are limited to ammunition already preloaded onto the loader drum, one crew member can activate and operate the entire system.

The system loader drum in the lower structure can hold 20 conventional 5-in (127-mm) rounds, or ten extended length projectiles with separate cartridge cases, or a mixture of both. It is replenished through its own manual load station or via the Mk. 6 hoist if fitted. The Mk. 45 is designed to utilize all current US Navy 5-in (127-mm)/54cal. ammunition, which includes a wide variety of specialized projectiles, fuze types, and cartridge case loads.

The firing cycle is relatively simple in operation and normal rate of fire is 20rpm. The Mk. 45 can also handle extended length ammunition, which can include guided and precision rounds, and these generally feature separate propellant cartridges. In this case the firing cycle is modified to include a double hoist and ram cycle before firing.

The operation of the gun and its loading cycle is controlled from the operators station control panel, which includes all switches and indicators required to select operational modes and monitor the functioning of the gun. In addition the operator can monitor the distribution of ammunition types in the lower hoist, loader drum, and upper hoist. The mounting utilizes the ship's 440 volt electrical supply via a power control panel, and a battery system is incorporated to allow completion of a firing sequence in the event of a power failure.

In US Navy service the Mk. 45 is normally paired with the Lockheed Mk. 46 Fire Control System (FCS), which incorporates an SPQ-9 track-while-scan radar, an SPG-60 target tracking and illuminating radar, and an electro-optical sensor system.

The Mk. 45 has been produced in several versions, the initial variant being the Mod. 0 as installed aboard the early Spruance class ships. This was replaced by the Mod. 1, first tested in the early 1980s aboard the USS *Briscoe* (the 15th Spruance class), which introduced automatic handling of different ammunition types and electronic fuze setting. The current production version is the Mod. 2, which introduces new microprocessor control circuitry and a number of other modifications designed to enhance its reliability.

Despite being over 20 years old, the basic design is currently being modernized and upgraded to fulfil a requirement for a near term improvement in Naval Surface Fire Support (NSFS) capabilities. This program relates mainly to the gun itself, which is modified to allow the use of advanced solid propellants together with conventional or improved ballistic projectiles to produce a staggering improvement in

maximum range. Structural modifications, including a lengthening of the barrel to 62 caliber, increased recoil length, and strengthening of major components, allow the Mk. 45 to operate at higher chamber pressures and to cope with greater recoil forces. The new 5-in (127mm)/62 caliber mounting is now being introduced aboard destroyers and frigates and is capable of ranges up to 63nm (117km) using the EX 171 Extended Range Guided Munition (ERGM). Using GPS guidance and a solid fuel rocket motor, the ERGM is capable of pinpoint accuracy even at maximum range and is intended to support ground forces up to 62 miles (100km) inland from a beachhead.

LEFT: A close up of the 5in (127mm)/54 cal. gun barrel of the lightweight Mk. 45 mounting. Its main function is Naval Surface Fire Support of forces ashore, as well as antiship and antiaircraft capability.

BELOW: This Mk.45 has obviously just carried out a sustained fired detail as evidenced by the cartridges cases on the deck and scorch marks on the barrel. It can fire at 20rpm.

Mk. 75 3in/62 Gun

This 3in (76mm) automatic gun was originally designed and manufactured in Italy by OTO Melera and has achieved considerable success in the export market. Following a successful evaluation in 1975, it was ordered for the US Navy and initially manufactured under license by the Naval Systems Division of the FMC Corporation. Subsequently orders were shared between OTO Melera and FMC. First deliveries were made in 1978 for installation in the first of the new Oliver Hazard Perry class frigates of which 51 were eventually completed for US service. The gun also armed some hydrofoils and US Coastguard Hamilton and Famous class cutters.

The fully automatic Mk. 75 3in (76mm)/62 caliber gun has a rate of fire of 85rpm and fires a 13lb (6kg) shell to a maximum range of 8.7nm (16km) against surface targets although it has a full dual purpose capability and is effective against aircraft and missiles. The gun is water cooled to dissipate the heat created by the high rate of fire and a tank type muzzle brake reduces recoil forces. The turret is unmanned; ammunition is stored immediately below the mounting in ready use drums containing 40, 80 or 115 rounds. Only three crew are required to operate sustained fire, one at the mounting remote control station in the ship's operations center, and two others replenish the ammunition drums. However, fire can be opened almost instantaneously against unexpected targets using the preloaded ammunition. Overall mounting weight is 16,500lbs (7,484kg).

Aboard the FFG-7 frigates, the Mk. 75 is teamed with the Mk. 92 fire control system (FCS), which is a license produced version of the Dutch Signaal M28 FCS. The twin X-band radar antenna for this system are installed in a distinctive egg-shaped housing prominently mounted atop the frigates bridge.

These ships also carry a SPG-60 STIR (Separate Tracking and Illuminating Radar) that can also be integrated with the FCS to illuminate targets for

BELOW: The Mk. 75 3-in (76mm) gun is unusually mounted high up amidships in the FFG-7 class frigates. Also visible in this view of the USS *Estocin* (FFG-15) are the Mk. 13 single rail missile launcher forward and a Mk. 15 Phalanx aft atop the hangar.

RIGHT: A model of the 3-in (76mm)/62 gun showing the below deck arrangement of the ready use magazine.

BELOW: This egg-shaped housing contains the two antenna of the Mk. 92 fire control radar associated with the Mk. 75 3in (76mm) gun.

BOTTOM: An SPG-60 STIR (Target indicating radar) aboard an FFG-7 class frigate.

both the gun and the ship's Standard missiles. Unusually, the gun itself is mounted amidships atop the superstructure so its arcs of fire against low-level targets are restricted fore and aft by the ships funnel and masts.

Mk. 38 1-in (25mm) Automatic Cannon (Bushmaster)

This the US Navy's standard lightweight gun system, installed for self defense purposes aboard many support and amphibious warfare vessels, is effectively a replacement for the 0.79in (20mm) Oerlikon cannon of World War II vintage. The gun is an electrically driven M242 autocannon, or chain gun, which takes its name from the roller chain that operates the firing mechanism and transports the ammunition rounds. Rate of fire is variable; it can be set at 100 or 200rpm in addition to a single shot capability. Maximum effective range is in the region of 8,202ft (2,500m). The gun is carried on a Mk. 88 heavy machinegun mounting and is manually elevated and trained.

Development of the M242 for Army use began in 1971 and it was adopted for naval use in 1986. As early as 1988 it was deployed aboard ships operating in the Persian Gulf and was fitted to the frigates *Fahrion* (FFG-22) and *Mahlon S Tinsdale* (FFG-27) during the Gulf War in 1991. The weight of the complete mounting is 1,250lb (567kg), including the attached magazine holding 150 rounds.

20mm Phalanx Mk. 15 Close In Weapon System (CIWS)

Despite the increasing sophistication of missile and medium-caliber gun systems, experience has shown that low flying aircraft and missiles can sometimes evade them and a need was identified for some form of last ditch point defense system. In the 1970s, the US Navy developed the Phalanx system to provide a short-range, self defense capability and operational tests of the prototype were conducted aboard the destroyer USS *Bigelow* in 1977. These were completely successful: full-scale production began in 1978, since when it has been widely deployed by the US and allied navies.

Phalanx is a completely self contained weapon system based around a standard M61A1 Vulcan 0.79in (20mm) multibarreled cannon firing up to 4,500rpm in continuous fire or bursts of 60 or 100 rounds. That actual ammunition is made of heavy tungsten or depleted uranium for greater kinetic energy. Co-mounted with the gun is a dual purpose search and track radar and an associated fire control system. When the search radar detects a target, it is tracked and evaluated. If its profile indicates that it is a threat then it will be engaged once within range. As well as tracking the target, the radar can also track the path of the cannon shells and this information is utilized by the FCS to correct aiming errors until the target is destroyed. Although maximum gun range is in the order of 6,000 yards (5,486m), effective range is 1,500–2,000 yards (1,371–1,829m).

The original Mk. 15 Block 0 was designed to counter low flying antiship missiles but the Block 1 introduced from 1986 incorporated a new search antenna to detect high altitude targets. The firing rate was increased from 3,000 to 4,500 rpm and ammunition capacity was increased while tungsten rounds were introduced. Block 1A offered substantial improvements to the FCS computer. Block 1B offers various enhancements including a Forward Looking

ABOVE, LEFT: A close of the rear of the Phalanx mounting showing the ammunition feed to the M61A 0.79in (20mm) cannon.

LEFT: The muzzle of the Phalanx M61A multibarreled cannon literally spits fire in this dramatic night shot.

LEFT: The USS *Ticonderoga* has the AEGIS class guided missile cruiser and Phalanx, a radar-controlled gun system. It is designed to protect ships against low altitude missiles or hostile aircraft that penetrate the fleet's lower defenses.

Infra Red (FLIR) and a thermal imaging video tracking system to enable day and night capability against small surface targets and helicopters. The need for this was demonstrated during operations in the Persian Gulf from 1988 onward when US ships came under attack from Fast Inshore Attack Craft whose high speed and small size made them difficult to counter. In the latest versions the M61A1 gun has been upgraded with longer and heavier barrels and additional bracing to reduce wear and tear, and to reduce projectile dispersion.

Despite weighing over 5 tons, the Mk. 15 Phalanx can easily be installed on any suitable area of clear deck, and can just as easily be removed and installed on another ship. Thus systems are recycled as ships, are decommissioned for refits, or placed in reserve. Over 800 Phalanx systems have been delivered and these are in service with 22 navies.

Phalanx is currently providing the basis for a new Inner Layer Defense system known as SEA RAM in which the 0.79in (20mm) Vulcan cannon is replaced by an eleven cell RAM (RIM-116B) missile launcher. The full range of radar, infrared, and optical sensors developed for the Block 1B Phalanx is incorporated in SEA RAM, which is currently undergoing development and evaluation trials with both the US Navy and British Royal Navy. The SEA RAM system is completely interchangeable with a standard Phalanx mounting and weighs some 900lb (400kg) less than the gun version.

US Marine Corps

Today the USMC is the nation's main "Force in Readiness" and is prepared to be catapulted into a war zone at any time. With major inventories of aircraft, armor, and infantry equipment, the USMC is a significant weapon and major part of the United States' armed forces.

With a remarkable record of achievement in World War II and beyond, the USMC showed itself to be the world's premier amphibious force. In the western theater it was involved in the major amphibious operations landing forces on the coast of West Africa, Sicily, Italy, Southern, and Northern France. In the Pacific it was the Marine Corps that spearheaded the drive to push the Japanese back to their homeland and reclaim the Pacific territories Japan had conquered. Operations such as Iwo Jima, Okinawa, Pelelieu, and Tarawa were bloody battles that honed the corps into the best combined-arms fighting unit in the world. Postwar it showed its strength in the Korean War at Inchon and fought with distinction in the Vietnam War.

Today, its current strategic role is set out in *Marine Corps Strategy 21* as "the continuous forward presence and sustainable maritime power projection of Naval expeditionary forces ... scalable, interoperable, combined-arms Marine Air-Ground Task Forces (MAGTFs) to shape the international environment, respond quickly to the complex spectrum of crises and conflicts, and gain access or prosecute forcible entry operations." *Marine Corps Strategy 21* also identifies a number of USMC specialist forces – such as Fleet Anti-Terrorism Security Teams (FASTs) and the Chemical Biological Incident Response Force (CBIRF) – which show that the USMC has a wider responsibility than amphibious assault.

To be able to achieve their missions Marines need to be able to move quickly to trouble spots around the globe, arrive there and organize themselves quickly and efficiently, and then fight as air-ground task forces—integrated organizations of air, ground, and logistic forces under a single commander. The equipment they need to do this incorporates, therefore, much of what the US Army and US Air Force need – tanks, artillery, infantry weapons; fixed-wing aircraft and helicopters – as well as specialized equipment for amphibious operations.

BELOW: A "herd" of CH-53D Sea Stallion helicopters prepare to make a landing during D-Day operations.

ABOVE: Two Marine CH-53E Super Stallion helicopters are led by an KC-130 aircraft.

LEFT: The black and red AH-IW Supercobra touches down to ground.

LEFT: The AH-IW Supercobra in camouflage colors.

FAR LEFT: A US Marine Corps AH-1W SuperCobra equipped with Bell Helicopter Textron's Advanced 680 Rotor System makes its first flight at Bell's Flight Research Center, Arlington, Texas,in 1989.

BELOW: A US Marine Corps AH-1W SuperCobra fires a missle across the desert.

ABOVE: CH-46 Sea Knight helicopters stir up a cloud of dust as they launch behind a CH-53 Sea Stallion near Yuma, AZ. during Exercise Desert Punch. This was a simulated helicopter assault mission involving over 60 helicopters from nine squadrons of Marine Aircraft Group 16.

LEFT: A US Marine Corps reconnaissance team braces against the blast of rotor wash from a CH-53E Sea Stallion as the helicopter lifts off from the Marine Corps Air Ground Combat Center, 29 Palms, Calif. The Sea Stallion inserted the recon team from 1st Battalion, 8th Marines, as part of the Combined Arms Exercise 3-98.

ABOVE: Two US Marine AH-1W Super Cobra helicopters from the 26th Marine Expeditionary Unit fly over the live fire range at Glamoc, Bosnia and Herzegovina. Assigned to the Strategic Reserve Force of the Stabilization Force, the Marines were taking part in Exercise Dynamic Response 98, a training exercise designed to familiarize the reserve forces with the territory and their operational capabilities within this region.

RIGHT: US Marine Corps parachutists free fall from an MV-22 Osprey at 10,000ft above the drop zone.

MX
01

LEFT: A Bell Boeing MV-22 Osprey comes in for a landing at the Pentagon to demonstrate its capabilities before an audience. The Osprey utilizes tiltrotor technology. Taking-off like a helicopter, its engines then rotate forward 90 degrees to create a conventional aircraft configuration permitting high-speed, high-altitude, fuel-efficient flight. For landing, the engines rotate to the vertical allowing it to land in helicopter fashion. The Marine version can transport 24 combat-equipped personnel or a 15,000-lb (6,804kg) external load.

ABOVE: A soldier cleans his M203 1.6 in (40mm) grenade launcher before a battalion live fire exercise.

LEFT: Navy Chief WO uses a GPS receiver to calculate coordinates for a amphibious landing at a beach near Makuto, Venezuela. US service personnel gave humanitarian assistance to flood victims in January 2000.

ABOVE, RIGHT: US Marine Corps Assault Amphibian Vehicle Recovery Model 7A1 arrives to take part in exercise Tandem Thrust 1997, a combined military training exercise to train US and Australian staffs in crisis action planning and contingency response operations.

RIGHT: Marines perform a live fire exercise with an M-198 6.1in (155mm) howitzer during Exercise Tandem Thrust.

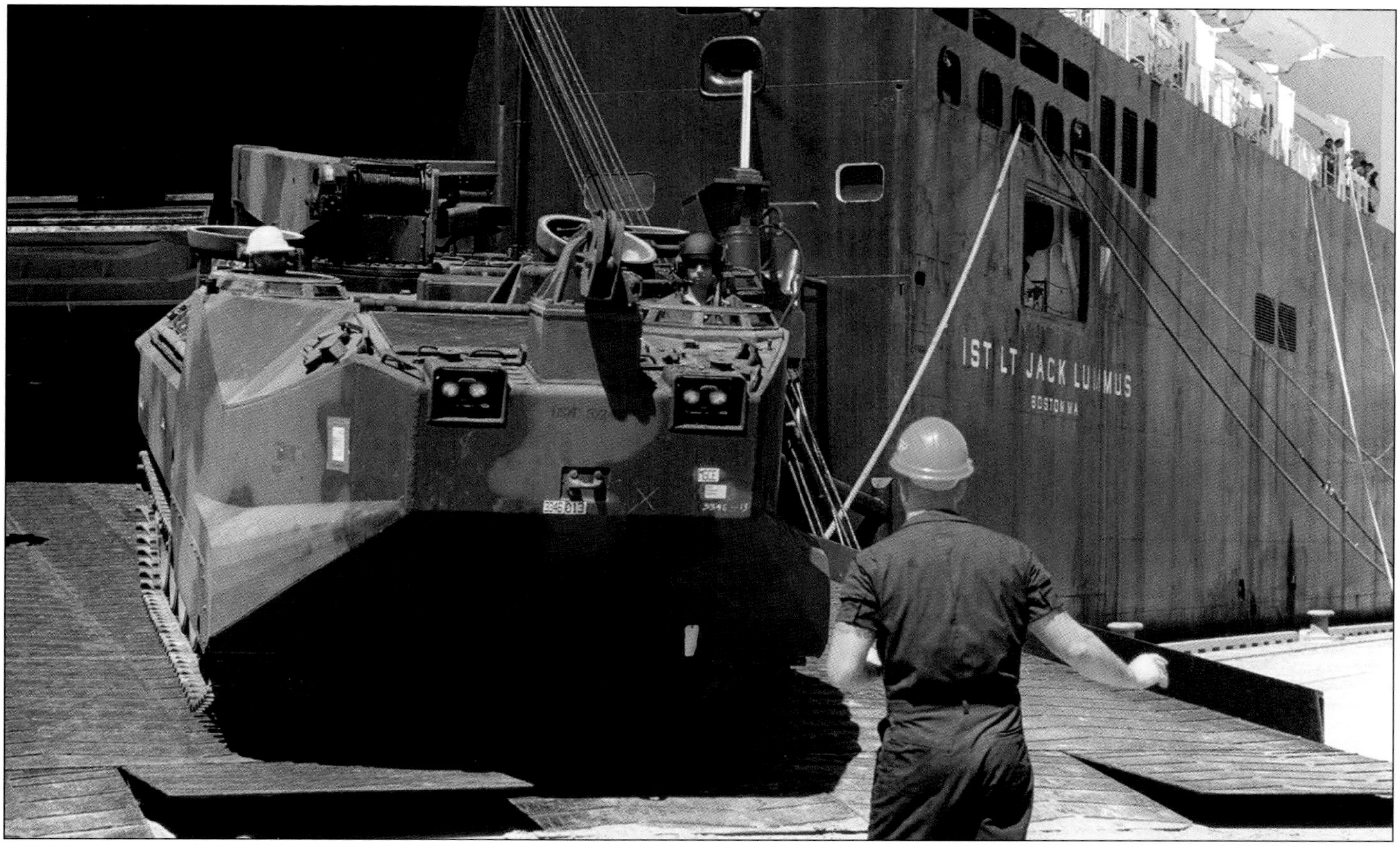
1ST LT JACK LUMMUS
BOSTON MA

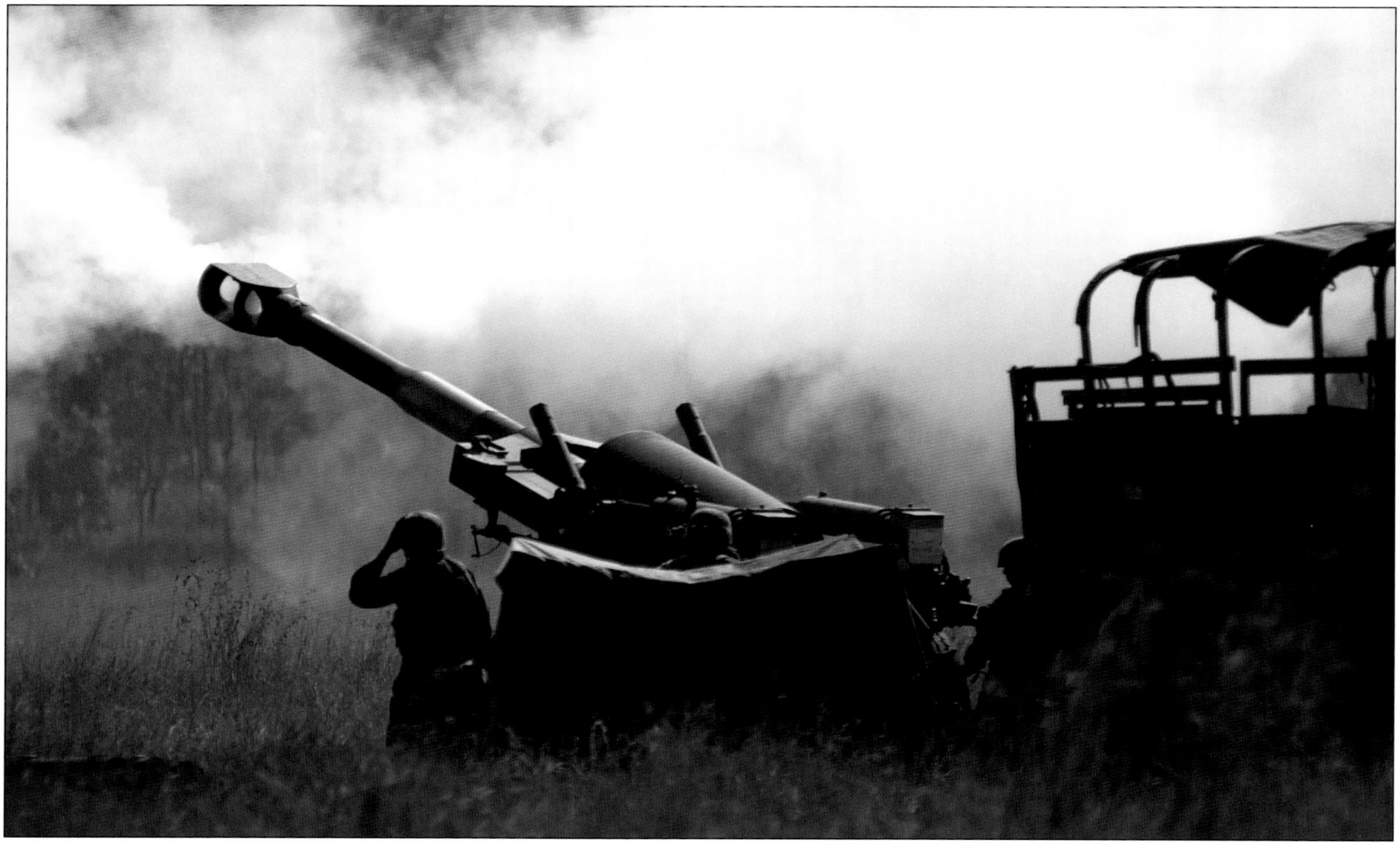

ABOVE: US Marines from the 10th Marine Regiment prepare their M-198 6.1in (155 mm) howitzer for firing while taking part in Combined Arms Exercise 4-98.

RIGHT: Two Marine cannoneers hustle a 6.1in (155mm) white phosphorus round to the breech of a M-198 howitzer during live-fire exercise. The Marine Air Ground Task Force exercise allowed these Marines of Golf Battery, 2nd Battalion, 10th Marines, to practice their desert warfare.

ABOVE: US Marines from the 8th Marine Regiment train for close quarters combat on the flight deck of the USS *Ponce* (LPD 15) during its transit to Liberia.

LEFT: Marines from Communications Company, Headquarters Battalion provide command and control via radio at Range 400 of the Marine Corps Air Ground Combat Center.

ABOVE: US Marines from Kilo Company, 3d Battalion, 8th Marine Regiment, 2d Marine Division, form a perimeter after unloading from Amphibious Assault Vehicles.

RIGHT: Marines from Bravo Company, 1st Battalion, 6th Marine Regiment, rush toward the target at Range 400 of the Marine Corps Air Ground Combat Center.

BELOW: Marines from Charlie Company protect the Advanced Surgical Suite for Trauma Casualties medical tent at the Military Operations in Urban Terrain facility during Urban Warrior.

ABOVE: US Marines on snow shoes patrol across a meadow at the Mountain Warfare Training Center, California.

LEFT: Two Marines try to collapse a billowing cargo parachute dropped from a helicopter.

RIGHT: Marines from 2nd Marine Regiment head back down to base camp at the Mountain Warfare Training Center, California as near white-out conditions set in. Marines are there to train in cold weather survival and arctic warfare.

ABOVE: Charlie Company Marines use a M-9 Armored Combat Earthmover for cover as they patrol the medical area during role playing at Camp Lejeune, North Carolina.

LEFT: US Marines from 3d Battalion, 8th Marine Regiment patrol the streets of Gnjilane, Kosovo. Elements of the 26th Marine Expeditionary Unit were deployed from ships of the USS *Kearsarge* Amphibious Ready Group.

ABOVE, RIGHT: A US Marine Corps Light Armored Vehicle patrols in the village of Zegra, Kosovo.

RIGHT: US Marines from Charlie Company patrol the Military Operations in Urban Terrain facility in a Helo Transportable Tactical Vehicle (HTTV) at Camp Lejeune, North Carolina.

INDEX

INDEX

ACKNOWLEDGMENTS

The publisher wishes to thank the following photographers and photo-libraries, who kindly supplied the images for this book:

Front cover photograph, and pages 131, 132, 133, 136, 137, 138, 139, 140, 141 (top and bottom), 142, 143 (top), 146 (left and right), 147 (top and bottom), 148 (top and bottom), 149 (top and bottom), 150 (top and bottom), 151 (top and bottom), 152, 153 (top and bottom), 154, 155 (top and bottom), 156 (top and bottom), 159, 160, 161 (top and bottom), 164 (right), 165 (top and bottom), 166 (top and bottom), 167 (top left, top right, bottom left and bottom right), 168, 169, 170, 171 (top and bottom), 172 (top and bottom), 173 (top and bottom), 181, 182, 183, 185, 186, 190 and 191 (top) and back cover photograph (main), courtesy of Hans Halberstadt;

Pages 2, 11 (top and bottom), 14 (top), 18, 19 (top and bottom), 20-21, 25 (top, middle and bottom), 30 (top and bottom), 31, 32, 69, 70, 71, 72, 73, 74, 77, 78, 80, 81 (top and bottom), 84, 86, 88 (top and bottom), 89 (bottom), 93, 94 (top and bottom), 99 (top), 100 (all), 101 (top and bottom), 102, 103 (upper middle, lower middle and bottom), 105, 107 (top and bottom), 108 (top and bottom), 109 (top and bottom), 115 (top), 116, 117 (top), 118, 120 (middle), 126 (bottom), 128-129, 143 (bottom), 194 (top and bottom), 198, 199 (top and bottom), 200, 201, 203 (top and bottom), 204, 207, 210 (bottom), 215 (top and bottom), 218, 220, 221, 236, 237 (top and bottom) and 238-239 (main, bottom left and bottom right), and back cover (inset, top and bottom), courtesy of Chrysalis Images;

Pages 9 (Chief Petty Officer Steve Briggs), 22 (top) (Petty Officer 2nd Class Ty Swartz), 22 (bottom) (Petty Officer 3rd Class Natalie Nolen), 23 (top) (Airman Justin K. Thomas), 24 (top) (Photographer's Mate First Class Martin E. Maddock), 24 (bottom) (Photographer's Mate 3rd Class John E. Woods), 40 (Ms. Grace Kelly), 41 (top and bottom) (Photographer's Mate Airman Apprentice Stephanie M. Bergman), 42 (top) (Photographer's Mate 2nd Class David C. Mercil), 42 (middle) (Photographer's Mate Airman Joshua J. Pina), 42 (bottom) (Photographer's Mate 3rd Class Martin S. Fuentes), 43 (top) (Photographer's Mate 1st Class Chris Desmond), 43 (middle) (Photographer's Mate First Class Martin E. Maddock), 43 (bottom) (Intelligence Specialist 1st Class Matthew C. Ruble), 44 (top) (Photographer's Mate 2nd Class Shawn Eklund), 44 (middle) (Photographer's Mate 3rd Class J. Scott Campbell), 44 (bottom) (Photographer's Mate 3rd Class John Taucher), 45 (top), 45 (bottom) (Photographer's Mate 3rd Class J. Scott Campbell), 46 (top left) (Petty Officer 2nd Class Richard Rosser), 46 (top right) (Petty Officer 2nd Class Andrew McKaskle), 46 (bottom) (Petty Officer 2nd Class Shane McCoy), 47 (top) (Petty Officer 1st Class Jason Everett Miller), 58 (Photographer's Mate Airman Tina Lamb), 59 (top), 60 (top) (Petty Officer 2nd Class Richard Rosser), 60 (bottom) (Airman Apprentice Mason Cavazos), 61 (top) (Petty Officer 2nd Class Michael W. Prendergrass), 56 (bottom), 66 (Petty Officer 1st Class Jim Hampshire), 96 (Lt. John McVay), 114 (top) (Petty Officer 3rd Class Christopher Mobley), 117 (bottom) (Petty Officer 2nd Class Charles Neff), 120 (bottom) (Petty Officer 3rd Class Heather Humphreys), 124 (top) (Petty Officer 2nd Class Felix Garza), 134 (top) (Petty Officer 2nd Class Jeff Viano), 188 (bottom left) (Petty Officer 2nd Class Gloria J. Barry), 196 (top) (Petty Officer 3rd Class R. David Valdez), 196 (bottom) (Airman Angus D. Stokes), 197 (top) (Petty Officer 2nd Class Michael Tuemler), 197 (bottom) (Petty Officer 1st Class Wade McKinnon), 211 (top) (Petty Officer 1st Class Spike Call), 230 (Petty Officer 2nd Class Felix Garza), 240 (top) (Petty Officer 2nd Class Jeff Viano), 241 (top) (Chief Petty Officer Steve Briggs), 241 (bottom) (Vernon pugh), 244 (bottom) (Petty Officer 2nd Class Russell Carter), 245 (top) (Lt. John Protz), 245 (bottom) (Petty Officer 3rd Class Jennifer A. Smith), courtesy of the Department of Defense/US Navy;

Pages 12 (Staff Sgt. James V. Downen Jr.), 13 (Staff St. Jon Long), 15 (top and bottom), 17 (top) (Pfc. R. Alan Mitchell), 34, 35 (top and bottom), 36 (top and bottom), 37 (top, bottom left and bottom right), 38 (top and bottom), 39, 59 (bottom), 144 (bottom) (Pfc. R. Alan Mitchell), 62, 63 (top and bottom), 64, 65 (top and bottom), 145 (bottom) (Staff St. Jon Long), 162 (inset left) (Pfc. Luis A Deya), 177, 180 (Spc. Cory Montgomery), and 191 (bottom), courtesy of the Department of Defense/US Army;

Pages 14 (bottom) (Cpl. Mike Wentzel), 17 (bottom) (Sgt. Thomas W. Farrar Jr.), 144 (top) (Cpl. Branden P. O'Brien), 162-163 (main) (Lance Cpl. Donald R. Storms), 163 (inset right) (Pfc. Andrew Revelos), 164 (top left) (Lance. Cpl. E.J. Young), 174 (top) (Cpl. Manuel Valdez), 187 and 189 (bottom right) (Cpl. A. Olguin), 188-189 (main) (Sgt. Craig J. Shell), 240 (bottom), (Sgt. T. M. Dale Jr.), 246 (bottom) (Pfc. J.L. Shelhart), 246 (top), 247 (bottom) and 248-249 (main) (Lance Cpl. S.A. Harwood), 247 (top) and 248 (top left) (Cpl. A. Olguin), 248 (bottom left) (Sgt. Jason J. Bortz), 250 and 251 (top and bottom) (Lance. Cpl. E.J. Young), 252 (top) and 253 (bottom) (Staff Sgt. David J. Ferrier), 252 (bottom) and 253 (top) (Sgt. Craig J. Shell), courtesy of the Department of Defense/US Marine Corps;

Pages 16 (top) (Staff Sgt. Jerry Morrison), 16 (bottom) (Kenn Mann), 26 and 52 (Gary Ell), 27 (top) (Master Sgt. Ray Conway), 27 (bottom), 28 (top) (Senior Airman Diane S. Robinson), 28 (bottom) (Tech. Sgt. Lance Cheung), 29 (top) (Staff Sgt. Cary Humphries), 29 (bottom) (Staff Sgt. John E. Lasky), 48 (Staff Sgt. Shane Cuomo), 49 (Tech. Staff Sgt. Justin Pyle), 50 (top), 50 (bottom) (Staff Sgt. Andy Dunaway), 51 (Staff Sgt. Larry A. Simmons), 53 (top) (Master Sgt. John Snow), 53 (bottom), 54 (top) (Staff Sgt. Jeffrey Allen), 54 (middle and bottom), 55 (top), 55 (bottom) (Master Sgt. Dave Nolan), 56 (top) (Master Sgt. Marvin Krause), 57 (top) (1st Lt. Dave Westover), 57 (bottom) and 67 (bottom) (Tech. Sgt. David W. Richards), 67 (top) (Senior Airman Greg L. Davis), 75 (Senior Airman Stan Parker), 82 (top) (Staff Sgt. Kevin J. Gruenwald), 82 (bottom) (Tech. Sgt. James D. Green), 83 (top and bottom) (Staff Sgt. Vince Parker), 87 (top), (Staff Sgt. Randy Mallard), 87 (bottom) (Staff Sgt. Krista M. Foeller), 89 (top) (Master Sgt. Kevin L. Bishop), 90 (Senior Airman Eric D. Beaman), 91 (top) (Senior Airman Greg L. Davis), 91 (bottom) (Staff Sgt. Efrain Gonzalez), 92 (Senior Airman Stan Parker), 115 (bottom) (Staff Sgt. Kevin J. Gruenwald), 121 (top) (Senior Airman Jeffrey Allen), 121 (bottom) (Tech. Sgt. Russ Pollanen), 125 (top) (Senior Airman Greg L. Davis), 134 (bottom) and 135 (top) (Senior Airman Jeffrey Allen), 135 (bottom) (Tech. Sgt. James Mossman), 157 (Tech. Sgt. James Mossman), 174 (bottom) (Airman Benjamin Andera), 175 (Staff Sgt. Jerry Morrison), 178-179 (main) (Staff Sgt. Bill Morris), 178 (top left) (Staff Sgt. Jim Varhegyi), 178 (bottom left) (Tech. Sgt. David W. Richards), courtesy of the Department of Defense/US Air Force;

Pages 23 (bottom) (Photographer's Mate 3rd Class Jason D. Malcom), 47 (bottom), 61 (bottom) (Photographer's Mate 1st class Mark Foughty), 79 (top and bottom), 85 (top), 97 (top) (Vernon Pugh), 145 (top), 158 (R. D. Ward), 211 (bottom) (Petty Officer 3rd Class Timothy Smith), 219 (Petty Officer 1st Class John Guzman), 228, 242-243 (R. D. Ward) and 244 (top) (Sgt. Bob O'Donahoo), courtesy of Department of Defense.

Page 76, 97 (bottom), 98 (middle and bottom), 99 (bottom), 103 (top), 104, 106 (top), 111, 112, 119 (bottom), 120 (top), 122 (top), 123 (top and bottom), 124 (bottom), 125 (bottom), 126 (top), 127 (top and bottom), 225 (bottom), courtesy of Military Archive and Research Services, Lincs.;

Page 85 (middle), 95 (top and bottom), 122 (bottom), courtesy of Military Archive and Research Services, Lincs. (U.S. Air Force photo, Department of Defense);

Page 85 (bottom) courtesy of U.S. Air Force, Department of Defense, photo by Paul Reynolds; print from Military Archive and Research Services, Lincs.

Page 98 (top) photo by Kevin Flynn, courtesy of McDonnell Douglas.

Page 106 (bottom), 110 (bottom), 113 (top), 176, courtesy of McDonnell Douglas; print from Military Archive and Research Services, Lincs.

Page 110 (top) courtesy of Military Archive and Research Services, Lincs./D. Moore.

Page 113 (bottom) courtesy of Rockwell International/Military Archive and Research Services, Lincs.

Page 114 (bottom) courtesy of Boeing Aerospace; print from Military Archive and Research Services, Lincs.

Pages 119 (top), 202 (top, middle and bottom), 205, 206 (top, middle and bottom), 208 (left and right) and 209 (right) courtesy of Boeing, and back cover (inset, middle), via Leo Marriott.

Page 193 courtesy of Ingalls Shipbuilding, via Leo Marriott.

Pages 195 (top and bottom), 232, courtesy of U.S. Navy/Leo Marriott.

Pages 209 (left), 210 (top), 213 (middle and bottom), 214, 216 (top), 217 (bottom), 222, 225 (top), 233 (top, middle and bottom), 234 (top), courtesy of Leo Marriott.

Page 213 (top) and 234 (bottom) via Leo Marriott.

Page 216 (bottom), 217 (top three), Raytheon, via Leo Marriott.

Page 223 (top and bottom), 226 (top and bottom), 231 (top and bottom), courtesy of U.S. Navy/Military Archive and Research Services, Lincs.

Page 224 Lockheed Martin, via Leo Marriott.

Page 229 (top and bottom) United Defense, via Leo Marriott.

Page 235 courtesy of Geneva Dynamics; print from Military Archive and Research Services, Lincs.